Love That Was ~~Meant To Be~~ Meant For Me

Love That Was ~~Meant To Be~~ Meant For Me

Shai C.

Vitasta

Published by
Renu Kaul Verma
Vitasta Publishing Pvt Ltd
4348/4C, Ansari Road, Daryaganj
New Delhi-110 002
info@vitastapublishing.com

ISBN: 978-81-991712-1-3
©Shai C.
First Edition 2025
First Reprint 2025
MRP ₹399

All Rights Reserved.
No part of this publication may be reproduced, stored in a retrieval system, or transmitted in any form, or by any means–electronic, mechanical, photocopying, recording or otherwise–without the prior permission of the publisher. Opinions expressed in this book are the authors' own. The publisher is in no way responsible for these.

Edited by Saumya Chaudhary
Layout & Cover Design by Rohit Gautam
Printed by Vikas Computer and Printers, New Delhi

Contents

Dedication	xi
Grateful To & Special Mention	xiii
Disclaimer	xvii
About Me	xix
Preview	xxi
My Pain Is Your Power	xxv
I Was Born By Love, For Love And With Love	xxix
Mind Warp: How Unhealed Hurt Shapes The Mind & Heart	xxxv
Gaslit: A match that burns the soul	xliii
All I Knew Was How He Made Me Feel	1
Case Study 1	10

Episode 1: Bruises Cloaked In Silence	15
Case Study 2	19
Episode 2: Where Love Never Knocked	23
Case Study 3	27
Episode 3: I Filled Every Silence, Still It Wasn't Full	33
Episode 4: Your Lies Were Louder Than My Love	37
Episode 5: Am I Crazy Or Are You Cruel?	40
Episode 6: Too Much And Never Enough	45
Episode 7: Why Do You Want To Leave Me?	49
Case Study 4	52
Episode 8: Why Don't You Love Me As I Love You?	58
Episode 9: Reflections Taught By Wounds	63
Case Study 5	66
Episode 10: Why Did You Leave So Soon?	71
Episode 11: Love That Led Me Back To Myself	76

Episode 12: I Know You Love My Body But Do You Love Me? 80

Episode 13: All This Love, Left Unreturned 84

Episode 14: Even Love Has Storms 89

Episode 15: Chained By What I Call Love 92

Episode 16: I'm Sorry for Who I Am—Or Was I? 95

Episode 17: The Question That Turned Into Me 99

Episode 18: Performing Love, Losing Myself 105

Episode 19: One Love, One Soul—Or Just A Story We Tell? 108

Episode 20: What Are You Trying To Teach Me ? 111

Episode 21: Words I Swallowed To Keep The Peace 114

Episode 22: I Was Never Meant To Carry It All 117

Episode 23: Wounds That Grew Feathers 120

Episode 24: Lit From Within 123

Episode 25: She Is The Calm Of The Night As The Moon Dims Its Light 125

Episode 26: I Was Never Really Gone 129

Episode 27: Is This Love Or A Memory? 132

Episode 28: The Quiet That Changed Everything 134

Episode 29: Tears That Speak 137

Episode 30: You Came Wrapped In Karma, Disguised As Love 140

End Face: From Prescription To Poison	143
The New Me: Thank You For The Pain … You Made Me Who I Am Today	148
Pain: It's The Gift Of Thorns	152
Conception	153
Poetically	154
Short Verses and Quotes	156
Beyond Meant to Be	159
Reflections	170
Acknowledgements	171

I loved loving you,
For it was meant to be ...
I loved letting you go,
For that was meant for me

Poetically Shai C.

Dedication

Sumit, Karan & Aranya—my reasons
Dad—my Poppy—my angel in heaven—my first love,
the only man who accepted me for who I am… totally and
unconditionally
My sister—who has carried more
than she ever spoke,
and held on to strength, faith,
and a quiet kind of fire.
No book could hold the weight of it all.
Your story belongs on a screen, with popcorn…
and yes… extra spicy nachos.

Grateful To

Nityanand Charan Das Prabhuji, for your blessings and support.

Special Mention

My mom, Niru, who has always been my safe place without question.
Sabita Mummy, for embracing my words with faith and steadfast support.
Hero Daddy for showing me that hard work is its own form of worship.
Lisa for turning a dream into pages, by pushing me to do this.
Roma for bringing light simply by being you.

This book is a testament of love and created with love by a dream team: Dipti, my literary angel—your faith in this story carried me through every doubt; Renu, my publisher—your steady support turned possibility into print, and dream into reality; and Saumya, my editor—thank you for seeing the heart of the work and helping it speak more clearly.

You don't have to love me—I love me
You don't have to value me—I value myself
You don't have to respect me—that is to be earned

You have to just make me feel safe—Emotionally

Shai C.

Disclaimer

The case studies in this book are inspired by real clinical experiences but have been carefully adapted for educational purposes. Names, personal details and circumstances have been changed to protect the privacy of individuals. These case studies are fictionalised composites and should not be interpreted as descriptions of actual clients.

This book is not intended to provide therapy or medical advice, nor does it establish a therapeutic relationship between the reader and the author. If you are struggling with your mental health, please seek support from a qualified mental health professional. If you are in crisis or feel unsafe, call your local emergency number immediately or reach out to a crisis hotline in your area.

As a practitioner trained in psychotherapy, I work closely with doctors and mental health professionals. The individuals in these case studies were referred to me through that collaborative network and their care has always been guided by a team approach rooted in compassion and ethics.

This book is about healing and the power we each carry—especially in our most broken moments—to rise, reclaim and rebuild.

About Me

I am Shai C, a skilled Emotionologist. From giving multiple talks and hosting self-love workshops, I decided it was time to pen it all down. This book is not a bible for successful relationships; rather, it offers directions to help you find your way out of the maze you have created in that beautiful brain of yours.

Our thoughts are the anchors to our behaviours, guided by emotions, followed by sensations and ultimately transformed into actions. This game of *mindception* can take you down a rabbit hole burying you deep into your own headspace. Finally, when you get out, you discover this game of deception comes from you, by you…to you.

It is time to ask your mind to get out of your own way.

I'm here to have you understand that you asked to be loved, not mind-screwed and it's time that I have your mind start making love to you instead.

I hope you enjoy reading this just as much as I enjoyed writing it.

Preview

It was a long journey. At least in her mind it was. To reach the point she had—there had been countless challenges and obstacles along the way. Struggle and strife followed her like loyal companions consistently through these phases. At a point, she felt helpless, hopeless and faithless. It hurt. The moments manifested pain. Each time, she succumbed further into an abyss of loss—loss of belief, loss of life's purpose and, more so, a loss of herself. What was life trying to tell her? What was the message? What was meant to be learned through pain and challenges?

Many told her it was a self-created path to destruction—her quest to seek love. From one relationship to the next—partner, boyfriend, or lover—there was always a deep need for acceptance and validation. With that came the urge to please, no matter the cost. This included risking her self-respect, sacrificing her self-worth and even losing her self-confidence. Each heartbreak chipping away a little more of herself until the wounds were open and healing seemed harder than ever imaginable.

She wrote it off as *karma*. For many, karma is just a word, but for her, it was an entity that played the biggest role in her life. You could say karma was her soulmate—her true love, true guiding force and in many ways, the determining factor to most of her ill-fated decisions.

Love was all she desired—to love and to be loved, as simple as that. But it felt so beyond her reach and this was the only thing she didn't understand—possibly the only thing she would never truly receive. Her idea of love was a fairytale, a fantasy which she perceived to be a reality. From Hollywood to Bollywood, love was supposed to be tragic, for if it wasn't, then it wasn't love.

Love was pain, love was trauma, love was meant to destroy her.

She never held a grudge against anyone who didn't love her back. Every time, she let it damage her—and each time, it cut a little deeper. But what she did not know at the time was that for every person that took a piece of her, she would rebuild herself one day. She would rise from the ashes, mend her gashes, evolve, then turn into a force to reckon with.

This is the story of a journey—not one where you simply find yourself, but one where you uncover the raw truth of love, of pain and ultimately, of life.

This is *my* story—a journey of acceptance, understanding and eventually, surrender. Surrender to the purpose of life by comprehending the lessons meant to be learned and how it can lead one to the gateway of *eudaimonia*—human flourishing, prosperity and blessedness.

This book is about love.

Self-love and finding the perfect balance in love—*Within you. From you. To you.*

The road to self-love isn't easy—it starts with pain. But that pain is what helps you find your way back to yourself.

A journey of tough love.

But once you're there, the new you, the love you feel will be all you need.

I am a poet, believer in songs, in melodies, in the rhythmic beats of words that shape verses of pain, deep love and self-love.

This book is a guide of processing your pain into strength, by using my pain as your power.

My Pain Is Your Power

For her true love was her soul
Her pain was her superpower

Pain is a language we all understand, yet we spend so much of our lives trying to escape it. We run from it, try to numb it, drown it out with distractions and pretend it does not exist. Pain is powerful. If only we allow it to become our strength.

There are so many ways pain shows its persistence. For pain has a way of finding us, no matter how far we try to go.

I know this because I tried to outrun mine. Time and time again, I would find a way to hide the pain and escape. I thought if I moved fast enough—if I loved hard enough, worked tirelessly enough and proved my worth to the world—at my expense (of course), then maybe, just maybe, the pain would disappear and be replaced with a version of validation. To begin with, it would give temporary relief. And gradually, the ache of that broken relationship, of disappointment and rejection, would simply fade.

Pain, however, does not work like that. No matter how much you try to run away from it or avoid it, sooner or later it resurfaces and catches you once again. It is something to be felt—fully, heartily, deeply, even when it threatens to consume you. For only then does pain begin to manifest into power. Paradoxically, then it loses its strength and becomes *your power.*

What I didn't realise then and what I want you to understand now, is that pain is not your enemy. It is not a curse, nor is it a sign that you are weak or unworthy. Pain is a doorway to your power. It forms the foundation of self-empowerment. As controversial as that may sound, once pain is processed, healed and understood, your nervous system becomes resilient—and so do you.

Every tear you've cried, every moment of heartbreak, every time you've questioned your worth—none of it was in vain. It was preparing you, strengthening and sharpening you. Because in the depths of your pain, there is an unshakable power waiting to rise.

This book is not just about love, relationships or heartbreak. It is about the transformation that happens in the spaces in between. It is about learning that self-love is a revolution—an intentional commitment made for you and by you.

You will see how healing is not a destination, but a journey. Pain—the very thing you wish you could erase—is the key to unlocking a strength you never lacked.

They say you have to learn to crawl before you walk, walk before you run and run before you jump. And if you want to fly? Well, you have to master them all. But what if patience isn't your strong point? What if the thought of waiting, of taking slow and measured steps, feels unbearable?

I wanted to fly—I wanted it all. And I wanted it *now*. For me, everything was about immediate gratification. I wasn't afraid of hard work; in fact, I was willing to push myself harder than anyone else. But I needed to *see* the results, *feel* the progress and *know* that my efforts weren't in vain. Slow and steady wasn't my way. I craved the fast track to love, to success, to healing—to life itself.

But life has a way of humbling even the most determined

souls. And what I would come to learn—through love, through relationships, through heartbreak and pain—is that some things simply cannot be rushed. Some lessons require patience. Some healing takes time. And sometimes, the only way to truly soar is to surrender to the journey—no matter how long it takes.

This is my story. A story of self-love, of relationships that shaped me, of pain that nearly broke me and of the lessons that ultimately set me free.

> Why do we seek an immediate return? Why do we want instant gratification? Why do we impulsively desire to have the reaction within the split second of the action?

We may never find answers to these questions. Only our experience can guide us.

We grew up hearing phrases like 'Good things come to those who wait' and 'We save the best for last'. Yet these words often fall on deaf ears—we hear them, but rarely do we truly take them to heart.

Learning to be patient was probably one of the most difficult un-learnings one has to do. Yes, it's a paradox—the beauty in unlearning the learning. But let's keep that conversation for later. For me, I had to first learn to imbibe the art of restraint, forbearance, tolerance and most of all—resistance—the ability not to be affected by something, especially adversely.

There are many aspects that need to be considered when you are trying to develop resistance in a positive and powerful manner. One of the first and most important elements is understanding that you resist not because you fear change, but rather because you fear loss. At this point, you may ask yourself what is it that you are actually afraid of losing ?

When someone resists change, it's often because they fear losing what feels comfortable and safe. But what if I was to say that the highest form of growth comes from challenging self-safety and self-comfort? It is very important to be in a safe and secure environment, but it is just as important to know that choosing safety should not be at the expense of your own growth and of your own evolution.

This was the understanding I needed—and ultimately, what I put to the test. With small changes in the early stages, I began to shift my mindset: the way I interacted with others, the way I engaged in conversations, and the thought patterns that shaped those exchanges. Gradually, it transformed the connections I formed with the people around me.

As these altered experiences became increasingly apparent, my desire for an instantaneous outcome began to decrease. I cherished and treasured the process rather than trying to force the results.

Suddenly, flying didn't feel as thrilling as crawling. And with that, a new mindset around relationships began to take shape. I was ready to embark on a journey where I wanted to proactively go step-by-step with my partner, knowing that it was not as much about where we ended up, rather about how connected we were in getting there. I wanted to move as slow as I could so that I could focus more on the present rather than on the future.

When you begin to see yourself as you are in the present moment, you start to view yourself through an incredible lens—one that brings both pride and tenderness.

Pride for who you are in that given moment and endearment for how much effort it took for you to get there. And this is the beauty of moving slowly—taking it all in, enjoying the process of who you have become.

But before we discuss who I became…let's see how we got there. And for that, we need to start at the beginning.

I Was Born By Love, For Love And With Love

I was born by love, for love and with love. When I look at my parents, I see a love story that can be equated to a fairytale. Now as wonderful as it sounds, it can also be truly terrifying. Terrifying because when exposed to a love like that, the all-consuming form—you seek it, you want it and you need it. And it would be an understatement to say, that I needed it so badly. I was addicted to finding it. It was like a craving.

I was a relationship addict. And relationships, provide as much as they deplete, they support as much as they drain, they pleasure as much as they pain.

> *I was so focused on each relationship I had, but never paid attention to the most important one—the one relationship that I had with myself.*

But that is now firmly in the past. There is no more sacrificing of myself to the gods of the bluest days. I have learnt my lesson. This is the story of a relationship addict, of someone who just needed love because she had so much of it to give. This is the story of my life.

My body craves your touch,
A hand to hold.
My soul is fed by your being,
Insides burning cold.
With every breath I asked to be loved,
Instead, you took my whole and left me with none.

Relationships. Are they simple? No, not at all. Yet we want them—desperately. Like a drug, we crave them. We feel lost without them, empty.

In my experience, relationships can sometimes destroy you. Especially, if they are of the following types:

The mind warp: This happens when a relationship has the power to distort your inner senses, making you question yourself and your own thoughts in ways unimaginable. It's not just confusion; it's a complete unravelling of your reality, where manipulation seeps into your mind so deeply that you begin to lose your sense of truth.

The mind fuck: A disturbing or extremely confusing experience, particularly one rooted in deliberate psychological manipulation. It's the kind of torment that doesn't just break you—it reshapes you, forcing you to confront parts of yourself you never wanted to see.

This book is going to address multiple manipulation tactics your brain has been using on you. Given that the mind is the only organ that can live in the past or the future, it is quite amazing how much of it affects the present. Each organ in our system, each cell in our body down to the molecules and the atoms ... the mind fucks us in so many ways.

I will take you through my personal experiences—of pain and heartbreak, challenges and struggles, loss and sorrow, trials and growth. These moments were deeply personal and emotional, touching my spirit and testing my mind. I felt them in my body, carried them in my soul and slowly made sense of them in my mind. It's all my pain—and hopefully my pain will give you strength.

Four letter words, ruling through life,
Pain, loss, hurt, cuts deep like a knife.
In from the body through to the soul,
Burning inside, the mind loses control.

How many relationships have you lost to mind fucking? It is actually amazing how our mind takes control and alters our reality. It has the ability to create something from nothing, manifesting it into a truth, from which we cannot escape. The main question is: do we have the ability to tell our thoughts that we are not going to allow them to control us anymore?

I believe we do, because I was that girl, that girl who refused to accept that her thoughts were not facts. I was the girl who threw away many good relationships and friendships believing that I was being disrespected, taken advantage of and disregarded.

I am not asking you to control your thoughts. I am just asking you to not let your thoughts control you. That is where the mind torture lies. So now we will begin this journey, the journey of regaining our super power and taking control.

***

For most of my life, I sought completion through others. I thought the right relationship would heal me, that love from someone else would fix the wounds I had carried for so long. But each time a relationship ended, I was left feeling emptier than before. I told myself I had simply chosen the wrong person, that I needed to try harder, love better, be more desirable. The truth, however, was that I didn't need someone to complete me—I needed to complete myself. And the way to do that wasn't to withdraw from love but to redefine my understanding of relationships.

Every relationship I've ever been in taught me something about self-love—even the ones that almost broke me.

The toxic relationships showed me where I had abandoned myself, where I had given too much without expecting anything in return. The unrequited love relationships revealed my tendency to place my worth in someone else's hands. The fleeting connections reminded me that I was capable of passion but that love had to be rooted in something deeper. I started to see relationships as lessons rather than lifelines.

Instead of using them to escape my own insecurities, I leaned into them to understand myself better. I asked myself what each experience revealed about how I saw myself. Was I giving from a place of abundance or from a place of lack? Did I feel safe to be my true self, or was I performing for love?

The more I reflected, the more I realised that self-love wasn't about cutting people off or becoming entirely self-reliant—it was about choosing relationships that aligned with my highest self.

For a long time, I thought setting boundaries meant pushing people away. But I learned that boundaries are not walls; they are bridges. They allow love to flow freely while protecting the integrity of the self. I started practising self-love in my relationships by saying 'no' when something didn't align with my values; by walking away from relationships that drained me rather than nourished me; by communicating my needs without guilt or fear of abandonment; and by choosing partners and friends who saw my worth, even when I struggled to see it myself. The more I honoured my own needs, the deeper my relationships became.

> *Love wasn't something I had to chase anymore—it was something I naturally attracted by showing up fully as myself.*

Self-love is not a lonely journey. It's woven into every interaction I have, every person I meet, and every moment I choose myself instead of settling for less.

Relationships have been my greatest challenge, but they've also been my greatest teacher. I no longer see love as something I have to earn or fight for. I see it as a reflection of how I treat myself. When I respect my heart, others do, too. When I value my presence, I attract those who value it as well. When I love myself deeply, I open the door to love that is real, whole and mutual. Self-love isn't about being alone—it's about choosing relationships that reflect your worth. And through that, you realise the love you've been searching for has always been within you.

Mind Warp
How Unhealed Hurt Shapes The Mind & Heart

What is this—the mind-warp effect in relationships? It's exactly what it sounds like: the mind being bent or warped. These are self-imposed thoughts that start to hold intense power over you, shaping how you see yourself, your partner and the relationship.

Over time, this imprint becomes an unseen force shaping your inner world, just as it did mine. It was not just the memories of past wounds but the way they rewired my understanding of love and self-worth. The pain did not remain in the past; it travelled with me, influencing how I moved through life, how I trusted and how I viewed my place in the world.

Without realising it, I was carrying the weight of that wounded child within me, her fears and longings dictating my choices. The survival mechanisms I had developed to endure the pain became my default way of being—creating patterns that kept me trapped in cycles of seeking love in all the wrong places.

Yes, our minds have this wonderful super power and the best thing is that it's not on remote control, but is as automatic as breathing.

We have a thought, and suddenly the damn thought has us.

It bends into its own reality. A perception which is so *real*, eventually manifests itself as a factuality. More so, as a *fucktuality*.

Thoughts become things. You've heard this before, I've heard it before, we have all heard this before. Yet, when it happens, we neither struggle with this nor do we try to dispute it; we simply believe it. Because our brain believes *negative* things, faster and ever so easily.

When it comes to the *'good stuff'*, oh my, we are left convincing ourselves with all our might that we are worthy of these thoughts. At this point, the mind suddenly has the ability to take over and prove us wrong.

> We are NOT loved, we are NOT worthy, we are WRONG, we are mistaken, we are BAD.

Have you ever felt that moment when your head hits the pillow and your mind starts spinning in circles? That vicious cycle—where what you think shapes how you feel and how you feel feeds back into what you think? An endless figure of eight—the symbol of infinity—looping through self-doubt and constant rumination, filled with 'what ifs and what did I do?'

Yes, that is exactly what Mind Warp is. The time when you actually think about everything that went wrong and even though it went right, it still wasn't right enough and hence *it was wrong because that's what you end up believing.*

It's scientifically proven that your brain starts to associate that moment—when your head hits the pillow—as the time to begin problem-solving and overanalysing. That moment brings a deeply ingrained, chronic pattern of mental analysis, driven not by truth, but by illusionary data and an overactive imagination.

Every night, as soon as my head hit the pillow, it started—the spiral. My body would be exhausted, craving rest, but my mind had other plans. I'd replay conversations from the day, picking apart a look someone gave me, a comment that felt off, a moment I wished I could redo. I'd lie there wondering if I talked too much, if I came off the wrong way, if I made someone uncomfortable just by being me. Slowly, their words—or sometimes their silence—would start to shape how I saw myself. I wasn't just overthinking anymore; I was becoming what I imagined they thought I was. It felt like if I could just understand it all, maybe I could fix it. Maybe I could fix me. So I'd stay up, night after night, trying to solve the unsolvable—how to be enough for everyone else. In doing that, I lost sight of who I actually was. My brain was convinced that it had to follow the same exact pattern night after night after night.

> Dear Readers,
> I want you to take out a pen and a paper and write this on it:
> Thoughts are not facts; in fact, they are not even close to being factual.
> Our thoughts are our perceptions, and what we perceive becomes a reality, and this reality becomes the truth.

Like a sinking ship slowly taking in water, this is where the relationship begins to lose its vision. Unfortunately, each of us carries our own truths, our own inner narrative—and we all fall prey to it, believing it's based on something real. But more often than not, it's a perception. And that perception quietly becomes the foundation of the relationship.

How do we alter the narrative and how do we actually come to a consensus and an understanding that what we are thinking is actually not real?

We do this by intentionally and purposefully focusing on allowing our partner to speak, to behave, to think and to act so that we can get to know their patterns better. Is it not amazingly unusual that we spend 90 per cent of our time shutting our life partners up by telling them either not to speak or try and convince them to speak, behave, think and act like we want. Eventually, we end up with someone who isn't their true self, but rather versions of themselves we want them to be. I would say that is the perfect recipe for disaster and disappointment. We cannot mould anyone according to our will—that is akin to putting unrealistic expectations on someone.

It would be fair to say—*I don't want to spend the rest of my life with only myself, I already know myself, I want to spend the rest of my life with my life partner. So why am I making them into someone they are not? Would I not want to get to know him or her better?*

***

Aggression was my downfall. I needed to vent, but was not able to do so in a healthy way. Instead, I projected or expelled energy that inevitably led to drama. A dramatic shift designed to spark the most intense moment—and for what? To inflate my value, through control, force and ultimately, self-sabotage.

There was a time when I had to admit something difficult. I had to take accountability for my contribution to toxicity. I was hurting people who didn't deserve it. My unhealed pain was actually letting me bleed onto individuals who did not cause the wound. Not intentionally—but still, it happened. I'd get triggered by something small—a reminder of a deeper pain I hadn't dealt with and suddenly I'd snap, shut down or say things I couldn't take back. I lost good people that way. Friends who showed up for me, moments that could've been meaningful—I ruined them because I didn't know how to handle what was going on inside me. My pain didn't have a voice, nor did it have a bandage—it was an open scar with a rawness so real that it came out as aggression, defensiveness and control. I wasn't trying to be cruel; in fact, I pride myself on the fact that I am not mean, I do not know how to be mean. In trying to feel safe, I built a safety net of protection, when what I truly needed was the courage to process. This detour turned me into a version of me that was unrecognisable. I became someone I didn't like. That was the hardest part. I said I loved myself and maybe on some level, I did—but the version of me showing up in those moments? I couldn't stand her—she was unkind and reactively aggressive. She was not who I thought she would be. And facing that truth? That was the beginning of something real.

Aggression is complex in nature. It requires fuel to survive and sustains itself beautifully, however, what we tend to forget is that the sustenance of aggression is at the cost of depletion of the self. We find ourselves fighting toxicity or any form of negativity with aggression, which by default, is the most toxic and negative energy. Hence, to negate aggressive behaviour, we use aggressiveness. It becomes an interesting paradox.

There is a thin line between aggression and assertiveness. The problem lies in this thin line—just as there is a clear distinction between force and influence. To be assertive in a situation is a strength of emotional intelligence. It leads to outcomes that foster calm, bring about resolution and restore a sense of balance.

Relationships survive on communication. Communicate to solve, to build, rather than to keep scores. We assume communication to be the speaking—the words we use and the way we converse. Yes, this is integral, but to communicate effectively, we need to focus on limiting our bias, removing our judgement and making changes to our inner voice.

The key to effective communication is receiving thoughts and non-verbal communication from your partner with comprehension and understanding. With each conversation, a new growth pattern is formed called episodic evolution.

***

There was this one night—I can still feel the tension in the room. My partner was trying to open up to me about something I said that hurt him. He wasn't angry, just…speaking with a sense of honesty. But instead of really hearing him, I was already forming my defence—waiting for him to stop talking so I could jump in and explain myself. I wasn't listening to understand—I was listening to defend. And I completely missed the point.

What I know now is that my desire to listen to respond was creating a blockage of communication.

I can still remember the way his voice grew quiet, how he kept looking away. There was no safety left. He could not speak openly and we could not move forward.

I bulldozed through him with my need to be right.

The sad part is, it could have been a moment for us to grow—a real, honest conversation drawing us closer. But I let my ego take the lead.

I didn't see it then, but that moment taught me something: every conversation is a chance to evolve together or drift apart. The choice is up to you.

The first step to un-mind fucking yourself is to allow your partner to speak and even argue openly and effectively with you. (*Effectively* being the keyword.) Let's be honest for a second:

none of us are immune to arguing or having moments of discord in our relationships; it is about having effective, meaningful conversations. That means there is a lesson and a learning in every episode—that we should be open to *growing through this, rather than just going through it.*

What I have learned is that we can even put an agenda to an argument, just as we do to a meeting. Write down with intention and purpose the objective of the argument and chart out a speaking time as well as listening time. This isn't about winning or proving a point; it's about understanding, resolution and preserving the relationship. When both people come prepared to listen as much as they speak, conflict transforms into communication.

Be purposeful in your communication pattern and speak to your partner, face-to-face and not through your smart phones. Smart phones actually make us very stupid sometimes. We do not need to argue via text or social media platforms. We must sit across from one another, face each other and have a speaker and a listener, and ensure that you reassure, validate and actively tune in to each other. The goal is not to win, but to understand. You're not fighting each other—you're fighting the problem together.

Gaslit
A Match That Burns The Soul

A virgin at heart, body was taken,
Looking for love, innocently mistaken.
He showed me illusions, I believed each to be true,
Only to succumb, pain and suffering of being used.
First to be told, it's all in my head,
Guided into darkness nothing to be seen ahead.
For I am the aggressor, a victim be made,
Not of me but by me, forbidden and bade.
Mirrors reflect a version where mind takes control,
Only to strip me, mind, body and soul.

All I Knew Was How He Made Me Feel

The drinking age is twenty-one because they say the brain is not fully formed and cannot process decision-making or have the right judgement skill before that age.

Yet, when it comes to love and relationships, there are no such restrictions. There is no legal age that determines when we are mature enough to handle heartbreak, manipulation or the emotional weight of loving someone who may not love us back. We dive in blindly, unprotected by wisdom, unaware of the lessons we are yet to learn.

Yet we embark on the journey of relationships as early as fifteen years old. That was when I began my journey of being mind-fucked.

At fifteen, we believe we know what love is. It feels like the rush of a first kiss, the thrill of stolen glances and the intoxication of someone making us feel seen. But what we don't realise is that love—true love—requires more than just emotions; it requires self-awareness, boundaries and the ability to walk away when something is not right. I didn't know this back then. *All I knew was how he made me feel.*

He was three years older than me. I was attracted to everything about him. He was a bad boy and it was evident from the way he moved, the way he behaved, more so from the number of girls that he had been with. But that didn't bother me because when he made me feel special—I thought I was the *one*.

Looking back, I see the pattern. The way I ignored the warning signs, the way I convinced myself that being chosen—even if only for a fleeting moment—meant I was different. I mistook attention for love, excitement for security and chemistry for compatibility. And in doing so, I lost pieces of myself with every moment I spent trying to be enough for someone who was never even mine to begin with.

Because when you don't heal, you repeat your actions. When you don't recognise your own worth, you settle for anyone who gives you a taste of it. And until I learned to love myself, I was destined to chase the same heartbreak in different bodies, hoping that this time, it would be different.

My central nervous system was wired for pain—for trauma, for seeking out negatives. My choices came at my own expense, because I had been made to believe that if I chose you, loved you, wanted you, it was because you were godlike. And if you loved me back, it wasn't because I was worthy—it was because I was lucky. I was taught to feel grateful just to be chosen.

You were my gift, for the men I chose were narcissists in multiple forms.

> Narcissism has a very wonderful way of making you feel like a queen before it strips you of all power.

***

The steps involved in the process of gaslighting are weaponised so beautifully that most of us who are the targets of this don't even realise that it's been done to us. Many times, we actually see it as a form of protection rather than ammunition that's tearing through parts of our soul, not to forget the mind.

The beauty of narcissism is that it actually attempts to make you believe that the version you become through this victimisation is who you actually are. And that is farthest from the truth.

The version you become is the one that is meant to protect you—protect you from the bullying, the lying and most importantly—the gaslighting.

So let me bring you to the four steps of gaslighting:

1. **Denial:** They deny what happened. Completely. Even when you remember it clearly, they make you feel like you imagined it.
2. **Role Reversal:** Suddenly, they're the victims. You're the one who's wrong for even bringing it up. How could you accuse them of something so hurtful?
3. **Blame Shift:** The problem becomes you. They tell you you're too sensitive, too emotional or just 'always looking for drama.'
4. **Mental Undermining:** And finally, they suggest you're unstable. That you need help. That you should talk to someone—because, clearly, you're not thinking straight.

In addition to the steps, they're actually stages of gaslighting where you become so broken and co-dependent on the gaslighter that you start to imagine that they are your support system. They are your protectors and your sole source of strength.

Eventually, you realise, that they are also the source of your pain and your lack of self-worth. That they are the reason behind your inability to trust in others and mainly in yourself.

But here is the truth. They may be the reason, but you are

the source as well. Not because you wish to harm yourself, but rather due to your inability to *un-see* what has been shown to you. To un-hear the words that were planted in your mind. To un-believe that you're imbalanced, unhinged or in need of help. But it's hard—because slowly you begin to believe what's been said. The rose-tinted glasses through which you saw your partner, the world and even yourself begin to crack. And somewhere along the way, you start gaslighting yourself.

There are two subsets of individuals on a general scale and within my practice, I see them on a regular basis.

The first are individuals who have been shaped by and subjected to narcissistic abuse—whether through parenting, professional dynamics or romantic relationships. The second subset of individuals are the narcissists themselves, who come for remedial therapy due to the victimisation they have faced at the hands of others.

Now this is a very broad and possibly controversial statement, one which might be met with a certain amount of angst, as well as possibly a sense of irritation. But that doesn't take away from the fact that narcissists, in general, truly believe that they are the victims. Their sense of disbelief is so deeply embedded that it becomes their reality—a truth they carry with them throughout their lives.

This is not to be confused with narcissistic personality traits. Here we are talking about narcissistic personality disorder and the intense level of cognitive distortions and beliefs within the system. When we were talking about gaslighting earlier, we were talking about a form of self-defence which is skewed and manipulated in ways that are foundational in the behavioural patterns of individuals as such. In other words, they do believe that their thought patterns are factual and in no way, subjective or influenced by any bias.

When you're dealing with people who constantly dismiss your credibility or invalidate any evidence you bring to challenge toxic patterns, it becomes even harder to show yourself empathy. Their behaviour is subtly enabled while you're left questioning your own reality—stripped of the self-compassion you need to move through and beyond the situation.

It is at this stage where the toxicity intensifies to the point of integrating itself within the system of the victim, prohibiting any form of survival without the assistance of either complete detachment from the narcissist and/or an exit from the relationship.

One of the most important messages or methodology of therapeutic guidance that is required to overcome narcissistic abuse is to actually reframe thoughts and recreate behavioural patterns that provide self-validation and emotional balance. To survive narcissistic behaviour, one must 'purposefully' and 'intentionally' (two of my favourite words as you will soon gather) be hyper-focused on knowing that a narcissist wants you to believe them. The only way to regain your power is through restraint, refrain and resistance. The restraint of reaction, the reframing of response and the final resistance to resolve.

I call this my *Six R methodology of survivorship* at the hands of any form of narcissistic toxic behaviour.

***

Narcissistic abuse imprints the soul. It is not necessary that it always happens through relationships; it can happen at any point through multiple individuals who play pivotal roles in your life. Sometimes, the pain starts in childhood, caused by people who should have cared for you. That pain settles deep inside and your younger self carries it without knowing how to let it go.

This pain became the lens through which I saw the world, shaping my beliefs about love, worth and safety. The imprints of narcissistic abuse did not fade with time; they wove themselves into my identity, dictating how I engaged with others and how I perceived myself. Love, to me, was not a birthright—it was something to be earned, something just out of reach—something I had to prove myself worthy of.

The longing that lived within my younger self grew louder as I did, manifesting in relationships where I sought validation, protection and belonging. But instead of healing, I found myself in cycles that reinforced my deepest wounds, repeating the patterns I had unknowingly internalised.

***

My younger self was in pain. She was holding on to sadness within her heart and a longing to be loved. This love was a need, building with intensity through each episode she went through. I could feel her angst within me all through my early thirties. Her calls were cries for help, pleas to fight despair—a desire to be protected. She was in a constant state of struggle, possibly even suffering, where the world was on one side and she on the other.

As a young woman, I would succumb to her fears and make them my own. Fear would transition to anxiety and anxiety would transition to defensive coping mechanisms leading to self-sabotage.

At one point, I could feel my adult state merge with my young self and the breakdown was significant. I began to cut myself off from reality only to live in a state of constant assumption. The assumption became a reality—no one loved me, valued me or needed me.

It became me against the world.

This was possibly the most painful period of my life. When you feel alone and you are unable to express yourself to anyone—you start living in fear—not the kind that keeps you alert, but the kind of fear that shuns you into numbness.

This was the point where I knew I needed to seek remedial support. My young self was crying for me to heal her, and I needed to do this for her.

Young self-work is similar to inner child work and this is integral to self-love. When we embark on a journey of inner child healing, it is essential to understand the trauma that has occurred. Not only what is subconscious, but what is also unconscious and conscious.

We have superficial trauma and this is possibly the most common form of trauma that presents itself through symptoms that can be seen. Therefore, it can be experienced and healed.

However, it is the inner child's subconscious and unconscious; the inner child's unrecovered trauma that needs to be addressed. You will find yourself consistently following cyclical patterns of behaviour and thoughts, leading you to belief systems which hamper the quality of your life. These systems are directed by trauma and are hence designed to protect and nurture, but unfortunately, all this happens at your own expense.

For example, if you are raised by emotionally unavailable parents, you will automatically become an individual who will constantly be seeking emotional validation and if it is not given to you, you will then start to believe you are unworthy of it. You will start finding faults within yourself rather than addressing the negative behaviour of others. This pattern of antagonising oneself is present because your system, your mind has been conditioned like this.

These thoughts and patterns, shaped by trauma, make you believe in cognitive distortions. They stem from not addressing the inner child issues tied to your connection with caregivers or the relationships you had during childhood and your teenage years.

Similarly, if you have been in relationships with emotionally unavailable partners, you will find yourself experiencing feelings of rejection and resentment, leading to an overall sense of unworthiness.

To fully love yourself, it's crucial to have a dialogue with your inner child or young self. This helps you understand the many relationships that shaped the adult you are today. The goal is not to dwell in pain, but rather to communicate, understand, acknowledge and finally validate your inner child. Make your inner child feel a sense of belonging, where there is acceptance of the emotions and thereafter, work towards reparenting, *repair-enting you to the state of mind that you need to be*.

How we treat ourselves is very different from how we treat others. We would be very different if only we bestowed the same amount of care and compassion towards ourselves. So many times, we have loved those who we know may not be deserving of our love, yet we consistently find ourselves second guessing self-love. The automatic thought is to question. The intention to self-love takes work.

Feeling loved is not easy. It takes effort and it takes courage. Effort because we need to work our brains to believe we are loved; courage because we must overcome our inner fears to sustain this feeling. And then comes the irony, the paradox, the most powerful truth—that love from another is not in our control.

We often believe we can control how others feel about us, but the truth is that we can't. No matter how much we convince ourselves otherwise, whether someone loves us or not or whether their perception of us is positive or negative, it all stems from them—their thoughts, their feelings and their beliefs.

> *So why are we so determined on feeling loved by others when our focus should be on feeling loved by ourselves?*

There is a simple answer for this—because our mind needs validation to believe we are lovable and looks for some sort of proof to validate it—usually proof from another person, for if someone loves us, then we have reason to love ourselves. But the truth is—if we love ourselves, then we give someone else a reason to also love us.

Love yourself—that gives a reason for others to love you.

Let's start the journey—from being unloved and lost, to being loved and found.

Case Study 1

She, Herself and Me
My Friend: The Toxic Narcissist

Introduction
Not all narcissism looks loud. Some of it whispers. It comes wrapped in woundedness, and cloaked in helplessness. It appears as someone who always seems to be hurting, someone who constantly needs your care, your attention, your reassurance. You give it because you are kind, because you want to be good. But slowly, you begin to notice how much of yourself is being pulled away to meet their needs. This story belongs to Meera, a gentle and empathetic woman whose desire to be a loyal friend led her into the emotional grip of someone who quietly fed on her compassion. What began as a warm friendship slowly became a space of confusion, guilt and deep fatigue. And yet, it is also a story of waking up. Of choosing self-respect over obligation. Of seeing things clearly, even when it hurts.

Anaya: The Friend Who Always Needed 'Saving'
Anaya was twenty-five. She worked in sales, wore confidence like a polished skin and had a way of making people listen when she spoke. But underneath the charm was something else—a

constant narrative of being wronged. She had been betrayed, excluded and misunderstood. Always. **Every story she told ended with someone else's cruelty and her own heartbreak.**

At first, Meera was moved by her. There was something magnetic about Anaya's pain. She spoke with softness, rarely raised her voice and yet she always seemed to make Meera feel guilty when plans didn't revolve around her. Her complaints were subtle. 'I thought we were closer than this' or 'I know I am too much sometimes; it's okay if you need space.' The words were kind. The tone was not. It always left Meera wondering if she had done something wrong.

Meera: The Empath Who Lost Her Centre

Meera was twenty-three. She designed quietly, lived gently and felt things deeply. She did not like conflict. She believed in second chances. She believed in showing up for people. And when she first became friends with Anaya, she thought she had found someone who understood her—bold, expressive and emotionally open. But with time, that connection began to take more than give back to her.

Anaya had a way of always needing more. More time. More attention. More reassurance. And no matter how much Meera gave, it never seemed to be enough. When Meera tried to focus on herself, Anaya would draw her back in through subtle comments or a silence that felt cold and punishing.

The Cracks Begin To Show

Things truly shifted when Meera fell in love. She met someone who made her feel seen and held her in ways she hadn't known she needed. Naturally, she wanted Anaya to be part of this new chapter. But Anaya's warmth turned into distance.

Her words changed tone.

Must be nice to be chosen. Some of us are just too much to love.

I'm happy for you. I just hope you don't forget who was there when no one else was.

Meera reassured. She included. She overextended. But it never settled. Soon, she heard that Anaya had been talking to mutual friends—saying Meera had abandoned her, saying love had made her selfish.

That was the moment something inside Meera started to wake up.

How Manipulation Works
Anaya did not shout. She did not demand. What she did was more complex—and harder to describe.
- She played the victim in every disagreement, always finding a way to seem hurt rather than accountable.
- She made Meera doubt herself, planting quiet questions in her mind about her loyalty and goodness.
- She isolated Meera by quietly turning mutual friends against her, using carefully chosen words that sounded concerned but were laced with resentment.

And through it all, Meera kept asking herself if she was imagining it.

The Turning Point
One evening, after another long conversation where Meera was left feeling guilty and confused, she sat alone in silence. For the first time, she asked herself a question that shifted everything: What would I tell a client in this situation?

The answer came easily. You are not selfish for protecting

your peace. You are not wrong for needing space. You are not bad for wanting joy that is not wrapped in guilt.

That was the beginning of her healing.

How She Healed

Meera started therapy. Not to fix herself, but to remember herself.

She learned to name the patterns, to say the words: emotional manipulation, guilt control, gaslighting. Naming them gave her power.

She practised setting boundaries. At first, her voice trembled. But eventually, it held firm. She stopped explaining herself. She stopped apologising for taking space.

She reconnected with people who made her feel grounded. She shared her truth. Slowly, her world started to feel lighter again.

> **For You, the Reader**
>
> If you are reading this and something in you feels seen, let that be your signal. Not every friendship is healthy just because it started with love. If someone constantly makes you feel guilty, small or unsure of your worth—pause. Listen to your discomfort. That is your wisdom speaking. You are allowed to want more ease. More safety. More honesty. And most of all, you are allowed to choose yourself—not out of cruelty, but out of care. The right people will never make you feel punished for growing.

Closing Reflections

What happened between Meera and Anaya is not uncommon. We often miss the signs of emotional control when they come wrapped in softness. Anaya's pain may have been real, but it was not an excuse to hurt others. And Meera's kindness was beautiful, but it was not meant to be exploited. Healing began the moment she stopped trying to prove her goodness and started honouring her truth. That is what this book is about—not blaming, but awakening. Not fighting back, but stepping forward.

Episode 1
Bruises Cloaked In Silence

I will never forget that night. I was fifteen years old, definitely blossomed to full womanhood physically, but mentally, I was still a young teenager. A curious extrovert who wanted to converse limitlessly, get to know people as much as possible—striving to be the Asian girl in America who intrigued the minds of those around her.

As an overachiever, I played the piano, sitar, tabla and guitar. I trained in ballet, jazz, modern dance, tap and gymnastics. I was in the choir, loved drama and sang classical songs. Being the centre of attention felt normal to me. I enjoyed having eyes on me, but I never thought that this mild obsession with attention could break me into pieces one day. This was possibly one of the deepest cuts that the depth of me would ever feel.

He was six feet four inches tall. Heavy-built, a chain smoker with minty breath and a deep voice. He was also a husband, whose wife was sleeping in the bedroom next to mine. He was also a father, whose son was asleep in the arms of his wife in the bedroom next to mine. He was my dad's best friend and he was supposed to be sleeping in the bedroom next to mine. But he didn't sleep, he stayed awake, he paced until everyone was asleep and then he crept through the corridor and entered the bedroom of a fifteen-year-old girl and shut the door behind him.

He was big and muscular, hard to fight off. He put his knees on my arms, sat on my stomach and pinned me to my bed. I couldn't move, I couldn't scream, I could not fight him off.

I will never forget the smell of his cologne, the smell of his breath—the frenzy of his want. He refused to relent for he was a monster in the guise of a man. He was evil personified. And I was his prey.

I never told anyone. I was too young to know it wasn't my fault; I was too mature to know my father would harm him to the point of criminal assault if I told him. So, I never told anyone.

This broke me. He broke me. The girl who once felt she wasn't enough on her own now believed she wasn't lovable at all. She felt like nothing more than an object of desire—something to be used and discarded.

Sexual abuse is one of the worst forms of abuse. It breaks you in ways that are unimaginable. From feeling *dirty* to feeling *guilty*, you begin to question your *own* self-worth. Suddenly your mind takes over and the cognitive distortions begin. They start with words that cut deep—*shame, filth, used*. You are not just a victim; maybe you are to blame. You begin to question your contribution to what has transpired.

Did you instigate this act? Was it you? Did you deserve it? Did you ask for it? Were you wrong? And now that it has happened, are you unworthy of being treated with love? With respect? Will anyone ever love you?

> One of the main questions I get asked is—*as a victim of sexual abuse, how do I promote and advocate sexual health and sexual wellness?*

How am I someone that encourages intimacy between

individuals and also speaks at multiple venues about sexual health being the basis to mental health and by default, physical health?

The reason is as I began processing what I went through, I realised it was not the *act* that violated me—it was the *man*. I was not meant to hate the act and loathe and despise intimacy, for that would only be reducing the quality of my life and my sexual well-being. Why should I not be able to indulge in the pleasure of sexual activity and satisfaction?

Many of us who have experienced sexual violence or abuse tend to avoid intimacy or shut it out from our lives. This is our coping mechanism and a perfect way to shield ourselves from any triggers that take us back to those moments of violation. But is this truly a victory? Or are we, in fact, losing a part of ourselves?

Building walls around us is in a way allowing predators to win. When we begin to abstain from life due to our trauma, it is a form of avoidance at the expense of ourselves. It is at this moment that one can say that an act of trauma does strip you of self-compassion. This is due to the fact that when it comes to our own trauma, we will always internalise the outcome rather than externalise it.

The trauma remains within us and will never be recovered unless we, with intent, bring it to the recovery level. If a friend came to us after experiencing sexual assault, we'd urge them to be kind to themselves—to give themselves the care, protection and comfort they need so that they can begin healing. However, when it comes to us, we automatically find ourselves escaping the internal trauma. We suffer by using avoidance as our main coping mechanism. We think that if we don't feel it, we can avoid facing it. But the truth is, if we don't feel it, we can't heal it, either.

We can never erase trauma from our lives, but we can learn to live a healthy and balanced life in spite of our trauma. And that is what processing pain leads to. It allows us to live a fulfilling life by coping with the challenges that we have gone through and *growing* through them rather than just *going* through them.

One of the most powerful skillsets we have as human beings is the ability to recover from trauma. This is not a learned trait, in fact it is innate, within each one of us. Our minds have the uncanny potential to alter our perception by purposefully using our own emotions. Emotions that are not processed settle in the recesses of our mind and within our organs. This is what is referred to as an emotional trauma suppression by either being taught not to feel in a certain way or training the self to bury what is being felt.

Therefore, keeping the mind and body trapped with thoughts of what we are feeling rather than just *feeling* what we are feeling. When we *think* about how we feel, it amplifies our emotions and causes a mental state of negativity. However, when we truly allow ourselves to feel what we're feeling, it opens the door to healing—softening the grip those emotions once had on us.

Case Study 2
'S' – A Sixteen-Year-Old Survivor of Familial Assault

Introduction
'S' is a sixteen-year-old girl who sought therapy with symptoms of anxiety, depression and signs consistent with **Post-Traumatic Stress Disorder (PTSD)**. She was referred by a school counsellor after displaying emotional distress, having difficulty concentrating and after changes in mood and behaviour.

Presenting Concerns
'S' reported being sexually assaulted by her eighteen-year-old male cousin during a family gathering approximately six months before seeking help. The incident occurred while other family members were present in the home, but not in the same room. After the assault, she confided in her mother and two aunts, but was met with disbelief, blame and minimisation of her experience. One family member directly accused her of 'making things up for attention.'

Following this, 'S' withdrew socially, began failing in class, and began experiencing persistent nightmares, flashbacks and displaying signs of hypervigilance. She also developed a deep mistrust of male peers and authority figures and reported difficulty in feeling safe in her own home.

Clinical Observations and Diagnosis

During intake and initial therapy sessions, 'S' exhibited the following symptoms:
- Intrusive thoughts and nightmares related to the assault
- Avoidance of places and people associated with the trauma
- Emotional numbing and detachment from others
- Persistent feelings of shame, guilt and self-blame
- Generalised anxiety and depressive episodes
- Distrust of men and avoidance of male-dominated spaces
- Difficulty forming or maintaining friendships and healthy boundaries

She was diagnosed with
- Post-Traumatic Stress Disorder (PTSD)
- Major Depressive Disorder (MDD), moderate
- Generalised Anxiety Disorder (GAD)

Therapeutic Approach

A trauma-informed, client-centred therapeutic approach was employed. Treatment modalities included:

1. **Cognitive Behavioural Therapy (CBT):** To help challenge distorted beliefs (It was my fault, No one will ever believe me) and develop healthier cognitive patterns.
2. **Trauma-Focused Cognitive Behavioural Therapy (TF-CBT):** To address trauma processing in a safe, gradual manner.
3. **Psychoeducation:** Helping 'S' understand trauma responses and normalise her emotional and sexual symptoms.
4. **Trust and Relationship Repair Work:** Focused on rebuilding trust in others, setting boundaries and developing healthy interpersonal skills, especially regarding her views of men.

5. **Safety Planning and Emotional Regulation:** Techniques for grounding, emotional control and developing a sense of safety in her environment.

Outcome

After six months of weekly therapy sessions, 'S' reported:
- Reduced frequency and intensity of flashbacks and nightmares
- Improved academic performance and school attendance
- Increased confidence in setting personal boundaries
- The beginning of a new friendship with a peer she described as 'safe and respectful'
- Ongoing struggles with familial trust, but she was able to emotionally distance herself from unsupportive relatives with the support of her therapist

She was discharged into bi-weekly therapy with a long-term treatment plan and was also referred to a local support group for adolescent survivors of abuse.

Conclusion

'S' demonstrated remarkable resilience in the face of trauma, especially given the lack of familial support. Her therapeutic journey underscored the importance of early intervention, trauma-informed care and the validation of survivors' experiences. Continued support and therapy are critical in helping her regain autonomy, safety and trust in future relationships.

For you, the Reader

This case highlights the devastating impact of familial betrayal and disbelief on a young survivor of assault. 'S' not only endured a traumatic sexual violation, but was further harmed by the emotional abandonment of those she trusted most—her own family. Her story is a powerful reminder that validation, belief and psychological support are essential to healing.

It also emphasises how trauma, when left unacknowledged or dismissed, can manifest as chronic anxiety, depression and difficulty forming healthy relationships. But with appropriate, trauma-informed care, survivors like 'S' can begin to reclaim their voice, rebuild their sense of safety and restore hope for the future.

Closing Reflections

When survivors speak, our first duty is to listen and believe. Healing begins with safety, compassion and unwavering support.

Episode 2
Where Love Never Knocked

Relationships hurt. They bring joy and moments of happiness, but they can hurt you. That's because relationships are made up of people and people cause pain. That is their primary defence mechanism. So, when a person feels even slightly agitated, they react defensively.

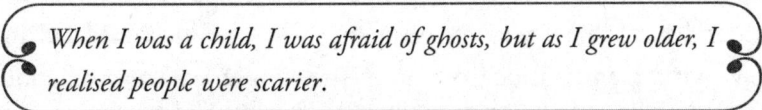

When I was a child, I was afraid of ghosts, but as I grew older, I realised people were scarier.

I read these words somewhere and I knew instantly that this was the answer to many of my afflictions. Now I am not saying I am not to blame, most likely in most situations, there are always two sides and two parties to the problem. In the end, I am also a *person*.

I was in pain. For most of my days in my young adulthood, I would say, I was in a state of subconscious unhappiness. Relationships were a major part of my life from the age of 14. I always had a boyfriend. I was always answerable to someone by default and by choice. It was the beginning of my own self-destruction. I never felt I was enough, just me, by myself. I needed a counterpart.

This started my emotional ride of self-persecution, my scavenger hunt for validation, and of seeking glory through the eyes of another.

And from this constant search for acceptance, a damaging way of seeing myself began to grow. Not only did I crave to be recognised, but even the ways in which I sought this recognition, eventually became toxic. I was burying myself to the point of shame.

***

Passion has always been a predominant factor in my life—especially, in my relationships and a driving force in how I viewed myself. If anyone would say I was pretty, I would state, 'No I am not; I am sexy; I am hot.'

I knew I was wanted; I was desired, I was someone you could fall in 'lust' with. But in my mind, I had already integrated the second fact, that I was not someone who anyone could fall in love with. Hence, aside from not being enough without someone beside me, I also had solidified a thought in my mind—that I was not lovable.

I had compensated for my feeling of insecurity with physical attraction and giving into sexual desire even if I did not want it. I was not promiscuous, nor did I have multiple one-night stands, but I did allow myself to be taken advantage of. I did it to feel 'loved'. For that moment of intimacy, I was loved. In my mind that's how I was lovable.

This had a lasting impact on my relationships and on those with whom I had the relationship. In the end, it was betrayal in the highest regard. Inevitably, one of us would betray the other.

And this betrayal would bury me further into an emotionless and bottomless pit of self-loathing, losing myself a bit more, hating myself a lot more.

When you begin to feel self-hate, you spiral into developing a belief system—one rooted in not loving yourself, not liking who you are, not seeing your own worth and, worst of all, not wanting to be yourself.

In relationships if you have this perception of yourself, trust me, your partner, inevitably and eventually will have the same perception of you. This will develop not because of his or her thought process, but because of yours.

Energies don't lie and they have the capacity to manifest themselves into reality. Most couples have a tendency to mirror each other subconsciously and automatically without the intent or the purpose to do so. This also works in the same manner when viewing one another. Though our narratives and perception may be different, the way our partners see themselves often shapes how we see them too—because our brain picks up on and mirrors that self-perception.

Now I know that this may come across as a little confusing, but the truth of the matter is that in many ways, our own self-narrative becomes the driving force of how our partner behaves in the relationship.

No matter your age or gender, none of us are immune to self-criticism or moments of low self-worth at some point in our lives. Most of the time it happens when we are in relationships and ironically, even when we are not in relationships.

What I mean by this paradoxical statement is when we are in a relationship that causes us pain, we tend to feel emotionally and physically invalidated. In the same manner, if we do not have a partner and we are not in a relationship, we feel that we are unworthy. It's a painful loop.

When you read this and possibly re-read it—it is evident that we are in a constant state of self-bashing. The question we need to ask ourselves is—*Why do we do this?* Could it be that our brains actually resemble patterns of an autoimmune disorder where suddenly we become the foreign object and the one that our brain begins to attack—*Why is our mind so mean to us?*

If you remember, I said earlier that our brains actually tend to believe bad things at a much faster rate than believing in something good. The way we need to tackle this is to be purposeful and intentional with our thoughts and actions and focus on what is right, rather than what is wrong.

We keep trying to fix ourselves without noticing the good in us. But we aren't wrong by default—there's always a reason behind why we act a certain way. What we need is to become more aware of our thoughts and understand why we're thinking them.

If a situation brings out a negative reaction, it is important for us to realise the trigger that has caused this version of us to emerge. That does not necessarily mean that this is who we are.

> *You are more than a circumstantial avatar, a trigger or that version of a toxic relationship.*

You are what is within you, and this is why it is said that the person who is '*yours*' will bring out the best in you, unleash the '*real*' you. There's a reason behind the popular saying, 'When you know, you know.' A woman's intuition is powerful. Learn to understand it and use it wisely.

You just have to wait and be patient. Sometimes, the wait does seem longer than you thought it would be, but it will get you there eventually and you will find for yourself, the peace you seek, not only in relationships, but also with yourself.

Case Study 3
The Love Bomber Through Rose-Coloured Thorn Glasses

Introduction

This case explores how emotional abuse can begin quietly within a relationship that first appears full of love and connection. It follows one partner's experience of losing their sense of self and later finding the strength to walk away.

How It Started

Priya met Aryan through mutual friends. He stood out. He was confident and generous with his attention. He listened carefully when she spoke. He remembered the small details. He said she made him feel alive. Priya had never felt so important to someone so quickly.

In the beginning it felt like a dream. He messaged her every morning. He showed up with gifts and surprises. He told her they were meant to be. She felt chosen and adored. She believed it was the start of something rare.

But slowly something started to shift.

What Changed
At first Aryan asked simple questions. Who was she with? What time would she be home? He said he just cared a lot. That he worried about her.

Then he began to get quiet when she spent time with friends. Or upset when she did not answer right away. Sometimes he would ignore her for hours after an argument. Then he would return with apologies and soft words and say he was just afraid to lose her.

Priya stopped trusting her own feelings. She wondered if maybe she was too emotional or too distant. She began to doubt herself. Her world grew smaller. She pulled back from friends. She tried harder to make the relationship work. She believed that if she could just be more patient or more understanding, things would go back to how they were at the start.

Aryan's Behaviour
Aryan did not see himself as controlling. He said he was passionate. He said he loved deeply. But when Priya began to ask for space or clarity, he became anxious. He felt afraid. Her boundaries felt like rejection. Her independence felt like distance.

He wanted to be close. But he wanted this closeness on his own terms. He did not know how to stay calm when he felt vulnerable. So he would blame himself. Or withdraw. Or make her feel responsible for his mood.

He did not understand that love without respect can still cause harm.

The Moment of Clarity
It was late one night when Priya typed a question into a search bar. She felt foolish doing it. But she needed answers.

Why do I feel like I am disappearing in my relationship?

The results turned up words like love bombing, gaslighting, emotional abuse. She read them again and again.

She was not imagining it.

She began to write about what had happened. She reached out to an old friend. She found a therapist. She started to rebuild trust in her own voice.

The Healing

For Priya, the healing was slow and painful. She left the relationship in pieces. There were days she missed him. There were days she felt numb. She questioned whether she had made the right decision. But over time, she began to feel stronger.

In therapy, she learned how to name her needs. She practised setting limits. She worked through the shame and confusion that had settled in her chest for so long.

She joined a small group meant for people who had gone through similar things. There she found validation and support.

She began to see herself not as someone broken, but as someone healing.

For Aryan, the process looked different. At first he tried to pull Priya back. He made promises. He said he had changed. But when she did not respond the way he hoped, he felt lost.

Eventually he began to seek help. Therapy gave him space to look inward. He started to see how fear had shaped his behaviour. He began to understand how control can wear the mask of love.

He had a long way to go. But he had taken the first honest step towards healing.

What This Story Shows

But it is also a story about courage. About the quiet strength it takes to walk away. About the long and personal process of healing.

About how the most important relationship is the one we build with ourselves.

> **For You, the Reader**
> Not all harm leaves visible scars. Emotional abuse can begin quietly. It often looks like love in the beginning—intense attention, deep connection, affection that feels consuming in the best way. But when love is used to control or manipulate, it stops being love and becomes something else entirely.
> This case is not just about a relationship that turned painful. It is about how people can lose their sense of self, one small moment at a time. It is also about how awareness begins with a question. A quiet doubt. A feeling in the body that says something is not right.

The Takeaway

- Real love allows space for you to be fully yourself
- You do not need to earn care through compliance or silence
- Feeling confused, exhausted, or constantly on edge is not normal in a healthy relationship
- Your voice and your feelings are not too much

There is nothing weak about leaving. There is nothing shameful about having stayed. Healing is not a straight line. And recovery does not mean you forget what happened—it means you learn to carry it differently.

Therapeutic Healing
For Priya
Priya began her healing by creating space. First in her mind. Then in her life. She worked with a therapist who helped her name what she had experienced.

They focused on:
- Rebuilding self-trust
- Learning how to set boundaries with clarity and compassion
- Understanding that the abuse was not her fault
- Processing the grief that came from leaving not just the person, but the future she once believed in

Priya also joined a support group. It became a place where she did not have to explain herself. Where people simply nodded and understood.

Over time, therapy helped her reconnect with her identity. The parts of her that had gone quiet during the relationship began to re-emerge. She learned to listen to her inner voice again. Not every day was easy, but each step was her own.

For Aryan
Aryan began therapy later. At first he came with questions—mostly about why Priya left. As therapy continued, his questions began to shift.

He explored:
- The roots of his fear of abandonment
- How his need for control came from insecurity, not strength
- Why his emotions felt too big and overwhelming at times
- How patterns in his childhood shaped his view of relationships

Through a mix of talk therapy, mindfulness and behaviour

tracking, Aryan began to understand that intense feelings did not give him permission to harm someone else.

He learned to sit with discomfort instead of reacting. To communicate instead of accuse. To care for someone without needing to control them.

Healing for him meant taking responsibility—not to get Priya back, but to become someone different for the future.

Closing Reflections

Healing does not mean forgetting. It means growing in a new direction. It is not about becoming who you were before—it is about becoming more fully yourself.

Episode 3
I Filled Every Silence, Still It Wasn't Full

It was easy to take advantage of a person like me. I lied to myself daily, so I made it easy for others to lie to me too. Especially if I was in love with them—for I had blinders on. It started at a very young age.

Maybe giving myself blindly allowed for cheaters to rise. I don't believe in the phrase 'once a cheater always a cheater.' I believe a lot of what you allow is what people will do. But I didn't know this when it was happening to me. At that point, as always, I blamed myself. I was the martyr in most situations, if someone cheated, which they did, I was probably the reason why they did it. And this led to damage beyond all control.

The first real relationship I was in meant a lot to me. It was the first of many things and it was also the first of a tremendous heartbreak. Girls usually assume that their first real relationship is the one—the one they will marry, the person they will spend 'forever' with and, of course, the only individual they will be intimate with. And of course, they expect the same in return.

Well, that didn't exactly happen. But the rest of it did. I found out I was not only cheated on, but I was cheated on multiple times almost weekly for a couple of years. In fact, there was supposedly no truth or love in the relationship at all. I was a means to an end. And the worst part of it all, I believed it was all my fault. Thus, emerged a woman so scorned, so jaded, so bitter, that aside from losing all faith in this thing called love, I spiralled out of control.

I began indulging and living life in reckless ways, taking out my anger of betrayal in ways that I regret today. I hurt those who didn't deserve it and I continued my faithless journey through the next few relationships with the same contempt—no one deserved my love, not even myself.

Today, I realise how cruel it is to react to torment with torment. At the point, I only wanted to hurt those that had hurt me with the same weapon they had used on me. The truth is—it damaged me further only—turning me into someone unknown.

What is life's lesson when you are the victim of infidelity?

It is hard to comprehend how something so painful could have a deeper message within it. Is it that we are born with soul debts and we owe time to individuals with whom our soul bond remains unfinished? Could it be that this lesson is telling us life is a mix of both happiness and suffering and denying either one goes against the natural flow of life? Could it be that we chose the wrong person? Could it be that our expectations were too high? Could it be that this relationship was not meant to last? Or could it simply be that we were treated badly and it is terrible but we needed to learn the lesson?

I honestly could not assess which of the questions above applied to my situation, but I do know that each and every one of them makes sense to me today. As a spiritual and karmic believer,

I will say that though I do not hold true *that everything happens for the best, I do believe that things happen to prevent something worse.* Imagine if I had never found out and I married this man. I would have started a family with him, only to end up in a situation of betrayal.

Lies stay with us, and no matter how much we may want to escape the impact of betrayal, we will have residual damage. Processing pain does not mean negating it in totality; it simply means that we shall not allow the scars to control our choices—present or future.

Just as I earlier said there are versions of ourselves that emerge during various circumstances, we also have specific selves that exist as well.

There are three selves: the public self, the real self and the ideal self. In relationships, all three of these tend to appear, but they have their own timelines as well as their own faces.

When we start a relationship, we often present our *public self*—trying very hard to please our partner, court and woo our partner and most importantly, keep them close. As we are portraying our self as well as having our partner portray their public self to us, we tend to believe that these are our real selves and the versions that will remain constant throughout the relationship. That is rarely the case.

Once we become comfortable in the relationship, that is when the *real self* emerges. And as this actual self takes form, this is when we start to question—*Is this the person I actually fell in love with? He or she does not seem to be the same individual. Why has my partner changed so much?*

In actuality, neither you nor your partner have changed. You have just become more comfortable with one another and, therefore, you start to become your actual and real self. This is the true test of the relationship. If we make it through this phase, we know that we accept one another for who we really are rather than for the image or the version that we were presenting to one another. At this point, we have come to the part of the relationship where we begin to understand one another and start to manage and accommodate each other for all we actually are.

As we continue through this stage of the relationship—which, keep in mind, can take years—we gradually become the ideal self: the version of us that creates the moments and memories the relationship relies on to survive.

The ideal self-phase in no way has no relationship issues. This is just where the relationship has come to be emotionally and relationally safe. There is comfort and ease with one another, thought patterns are less confrontational and communication is in sync with behavioural patterns, leading to a balance between the partners.

Episode 4
Your Lies Were Louder Than My Love

Guilt is a one-syllable word with great strength and power; it defines a human being in their deepest sense. Betrayal, a three-syllable word with great weakness and power, determines life for many human beings.

As I said earlier, lies stay with us, for much longer than we wish they would. They stay, they impact, they rule and for some—they become a way of life. If lied to, we will do the same back. Why should we not?

I have been cheated on and ultimately, I have cheated on people. Am I guiltless? No, I was jaded, I was bitter but mostly I was selfish. I felt the guilt; I also didn't care about the guilt I felt. For I was broken from the multiple disloyal acts that were committed by those I thought loved me. When you are betrayed, you go through multiple stages of emotion and pain.

When you are cheated on, a part of you dies; it is an end and you grieve. This is a natural process—just as you mourn the death of a person, you also mourn the loss of trust, which leaves a deep void within you. Whether you choose to end the relationship or not, it is a decision that bears no consequence on the feeling you have at that given moment. The individual you gave yourself to also gave himself or herself to another. And that hurts in a way that is irreparable.

Therefore, I was ready to forsake who I was and who I was 'in love' with at that time for a moment of passion, because that's who I had become—and this was not okay, but I did not care.

 How could someone with so much love to give and an individual who could never harm anyone intentionally, succumb to committing that same betrayal?

We become the people we don't want to be because we simply do not know how to not be them. The moment we stop listening to our inner cries and pleas of morality, we tend to slip into dimensions of 'us' that are truly distorted. When we do not love ourselves, we are unable to overcome moments of anger, frustration or discord within ourselves.

During those moments, phases and life experiences, our immediate thought process is to mirror what has happened to us by doing it to those around us. The amount of effort we put into building a positive environment—whether in a relationship or a friendship—can flip when we feel betrayed. Suddenly, we double that effort, but this time to create distance, negativity or to become someone we're not, simply because it feels easier than facing the hurt.

It is easier to be bad than it is to be good. It is easier to inflict pain than it is to overcome it. It is easier to do what was done to us than to be the only one suffering. But what we do not realise is this form of *easy* is actually the hardest thing we are doing to ourselves. This does not stem from strength and self-love, rather this behavioural pattern comes from the inability to love ourselves enough *by us*.

Low self-esteem and revenge enable us to seek love and attention from any means. These paths are unethical, immoral and possibly against all our values, but we surrender for those few moments of desire *and to be desired.*

Episode 5
Am I Crazy Or Are You Cruel?

She's crazy about you
You only see the crazy
To understand a woman like her
You need to be a man

Imbalanced, crazy, mental, hyper—I have been called many things in my life. Surprisingly the people who say these things to me are the ones whom I considered my loved ones: partners, friends and confidantes. There were times when I did wonder if I was mentally imbalanced, for things were always intense, whether it was love, anger, hate, resentment or most importantly, disappointment. I would feel it deep within my insides.

One of my biggest faults would be my inability to not react to everything that is said, or done or not done. I had to defend myself, I had to get the last word in and I had to respond. If I didn't, I would be obsessed and consumed with the matter until I did respond—and this was unhealthy. I only internalised this much later in life, when the meltdowns, the overreactions, the drama and the scarring had already taken place. No reaction is also a reaction. Silence is also a response.

Now aside from feeling unlovable and accepting being desirable as my fate, knowing I was not enough unless I had someone beside me, I also imagined that maybe I was crazy. And I was only sixteen years old.

This is a lot of baggage for any teenager to have within themselves. Today, when people ask me what I do, I honestly say that as an EQ mentor, *I am raising adults with less baggage.* I wish I had someone to guide me at sixteen and tell me that all those preconceived notions in my head were mere illusions and did not matter. They were not indicative of who I was, nor were they reflections of me as a person, but rather they were created and stated by individuals who had a lack within themselves.

Not every abuse, allegation, or assertion holds true, for most of the time they resonate the state of unhappiness within the aggressor and we take them on as a reality of our own.

***

Resentment is an emotion which leads to tremendous affliction. Not only upon the individual who is making the comments, but also consequent to the person themselves. Individuals, when in a stage of rage or anger, seemingly always '*forget*' what may have triggered such an emotional response. And this is where we say that the emotions take so much control of our mind, body and inner soul that rationale and reason become clouded to the point of actual brain fog. Our brain will switch off from the reason and only focus on the action.

This was usually the state of affairs within my life. I found myself reacting, as I always did, to situations that were unfair or unjust as that is what was in my mind. However, my response was always intense. The intensity was the flaw which needed amendment.

Whether the comments came from hate, envy, jealousy or merely from irritation, they were enough to trigger a deep response in me. It took me a long time to learn that a reaction was not always necessary and that silence takes precedence as a win in any battle. At this point though, you will have questions, and this is where you will have to find the balance between how, what and who to react to. You have the power to decide whether the reaction is even necessary or not.

You will ask yourself: If I choose silence, does this mean that non-reaction is complacency? Does it mean that if I do not react, then I am allowing myself to be disrespected? Is silence, a form of contradicting self-love?

The short and sweet answer is—no. Sometimes you just need to just walk away. I agree that indignities are unforgivable. I also feel the more you interact in the matter, the more you feed them.

Judgement is unjustifiable, but there are so many that will judge. What I needed to realise was that both aspects stem from hate.

Sometimes, you've got to dance your way through the noise and let the world's opinions slide right off your shoulders.

Haters will hate, but they are also your biggest compliment. It takes a lot of envy and jealousy to hate someone. So, take pride in the aspect that you definitely have something beautiful and brilliant about you to be hated. If someone dislikes you or accuses you of being imbalanced because you decide to stand up for yourself or for someone else, it is not your issue. It's theirs.

You are not crazy, you are not mentally ill, you are human, you feel. Choose your battles wisely, choose what you wish to extend your energy towards in terms of reactions and responses, but do not change to conform. I learnt this as I grew up and I wish I had learned it when I was much younger. It saves you a lot of useless self-persecuting, indulging in emotions of pain, sorrow and anxiety and mostly, fear; the fear of who you are and what you feel.

***

It is commonly known that growth comes from learning. But what if I told you that the most amount of growth can actually come from the *unlearning*? The unlearning of patterns, thought processes, of automatic impulsive responses and most importantly, the unlearning of coping mechanisms. We all consider coping mechanisms as our safety guards, our walls of protection, our boundaries, when in actuality, they are sometimes unhealthy defence mechanisms that prevent us from evolving. From evolving as individuals, who need to be evolving from a situation.

The adults that we have become are products of learned behavioural patterns from childhood, especially based on the relationship that we have had with those that have cared for us, those that we have socially been interacting with and those that have played any role in our lives. These behavioural patterns become our instantaneous methodology of response/reaction to any given situation or person. If you consider them today and compare them to yourself as a child or teenager, you will see a resemblance in that response and reaction. The way you responded to being criticised, rejected, punished or controlled as a child often mirrors how you respond to similar situations as an adult—those patterns become familiar, almost instinctive, shaping the adult version of you. The child and the adult are yet connected when it comes to the automatic behavioural responses to situations which are triggering.

It is these patterns that we need to focus on unlearning, so our systems become less familiar with criticism, validation, rejection and negativity and allow ourselves to feel comfortable with self-validation when invalidated, self-acceptance when rejected and choose transformative positivity when faced with negativity. We must create a sense of comfort within our central nervous system with 'feel good feelings' of belonging and a linear sense of self-worth.

Episode 6
Too Much And Never Enough

I feel deeply. I don't know how else to feel, even today. I feel with an intensity that encompasses my whole being. When I love, I love with totality, without condition and with so much potency that it overwhelms me at times. When I worry, I do so in a way that stress can overwhelm me, pushing me toward a potential borderline panic attack.

When I am disrespected, I cry. When I am upset, I cry. When I am sad, I cry. When I am disappointed, I cry. But… when I am happy, I also shed tears of joy. When I am nostalgic, I feel my heart melt; when I remember my father, I break down into silent tears. I am like a coconut—tough and resilient on the outside, yet within me lies deep sensitivity, compassion, endearment and kindness. The level of sensitivity is possibly an element that individuals may be fearful of. There were times I did not want to feel this deeply. Part of me wanted to be indifferent or capable of keeping emotions at bay, but I could not.

It would not be me if I didn't succumb to the experience. And if it wasn't me, I wasn't comfortable. This is another paradox in the way my mind worked, *I could only feel comfort within the discomfort of intense feelings.* The higher the threshold of emotion, the more I could feel what was needed, what was necessary, what was expected.

There were times where I would wonder if this level of attachment to others and the need to ease the pain of others could be due to my own lack of 'self-unmet' needs. And if this was the case, would it be better to distance myself from this form of behavioural pattern? Was detachment a better way of thinking and ultimately being?

So many avatars claim that detachment is the route to inner peace and happiness. I personally debate this viewpoint as I do not feel detaching one's self from emotions of love and care would encourage peace within the self. I would, in fact, say that this level of detachment creates a void within, unleashing a dry and arid inner landscape that strips away compassion and undermines the very mission of humanity.

Nonetheless, I do subscribe by the view that ultimate inner peace is dependent on the ability to channel emotions from weaknesses to strength. It took me many years to comprehend the uneasiness associated with my sensitive nature, leading me to react to all situations with exaggerated intensity levels. Those reactions took their toll on me as well as on those around me. Eventually I understood life's message to me. I was not meant to change the depth of feelings I had; my personality did not require alterations in the magnitude of sensitivity I possessed. I was meant to transition the self-sensitivity towards being sensitive to others and their situations.

We all have emotions, but the trouble arises when they have us. We all feel, but if those feelings take control of our senses, we break down. Life is our greatest academician from which we receive lessons deep and profound. We were born with love, with care, with compassion and with all the emotions we speak of daily. Life is not about deleting those emotions from within you; life is about managing them without losing their true essence.

I will still vehemently defend an ill-treated child, stranger or known person, and I will stand up for the rights of all those underprivileged or discriminated against. I will love without condition and with an abundance of fondness; I will yet worry if a loved one is in need and I will yet cry for both joy and suffering. No matter how many years go by, I will remember my father and shed tears of his loss. I will still watch a movie and break down. I will embrace all my emotions, for each of them are special to me—they are part of me; they make me who I am.

I love my emotions, I love the way I feel—intensely and with fervour. I will yet feel deeply.

I will feel the feeling, but I will not become it. One must feel, one must experience and then one must let go of it. *I will feel.* The only difference is today *I know these feelings won't become me.*

It is known that sometimes the best way to get something out of your system is to actually feel it with all of its intensity. Even pain, must be felt in order for the level to decrease. As human beings, we tend to think about what we're feeling rather than feel what we are feeling and in the process of thinking, our feelings become amplified. Why does this happen? If I was to ask you whether fear is a physical or mental emotion, most likely your answer will be that it's emotional. The truth is that fear is actually a physical emotion and what I mean by that is that it starts in the brain, but it ends in the body. Our brain will send a message, but the ultimate fear is within our system.

So, to feel with this intensity is not a weakness, but rather a processing power which can lead to a much better outcome. The aim here is to not think about it so much. When the thought processes take over and the cognition becomes priority over everything else, we are unable to forget what we are feeling. And therefore, we will continue to feel it until we ultimately break down. This is what is meant by 'our feelings having us'. Emotion, such as hate and anger should not become you. Sadness and fear should not become you. You can feel but that feeling should not become you.

Episode 7
Why Do You Want To Leave Me?

When your mind vehemently believes that you are not lovable, you exude a corresponding aura. And when this thought process becomes so deeply integrated into your mind and body, it consumes you and you are then consumed with the desire and a want to be loved. One is also deeply affected by rejection of any kind in any form.

My obsession with needing love from someone to feel worthy lasted for many years. The normal reaction to rejection or lack of reciprocity would be a few days of feeling dejected and maybe eating a few tubs of Ben & Jerry's mint chocolate chip ice cream, but my reaction was much deeper. I began to blame myself for the lack of love, finding faults within myself and eventually burying myself into a deeper hole of self-shaming.

I would assume I was either not enough or my acts of love were not. I would over-compensate by giving myself in entirety even at the cost of my self-respect. I would take abuse, forgive infidelity, indulge in immoral acts and mostly, I would beg for the relationship to not end.

This behavioural pattern comes more from fear than it does

from any other sensation. You do not want to lose the relationship for then it validates your sense of self-reality, which is that you were not chosen and if you are not chosen, you are standing in a pit of despair.

My relationships were special. Each one of them taught me lessons that I needed to learn. But at the time they ended, I was ensued with a sense of 'Why me?'—an insecure and anxious feeling in the gut of my soul. I would not view the relationship ending as being one that was not meant to be, nor would I see the individual as not being the one for me; I would only see rejection as a plethora of negative emotions and negative thoughts that took over.

Letting go and moving on were two aspects my heart was not willing to process as beneficial. For I was unable to process the loss as mere loss, it needed to be understood at the deepest level with the most self-critical and self-hatefulness lens.

As I type this, a smile does come to my face, wishing I knew then what I know now, that this was really not catastrophic. Today, I can see that those relationships were neither healthy, nor loving and certainly not built to last. Sometimes we need to set people free in the hope of finding the right person. They say that one of divinity's greatest blessings is unanswered prayers. I would assume similarly a relationship that didn't work out simply as a gift in disguise. It is to allow the *right one*, a more substantial and possibly from a spiritual perspective, *the predestined relationship* to ordain your life.

Relationships are hard and I am not saying I am in a perfect one, but I know I am in the relationship my heart and soul are happy with and with the person who makes me a better human being. This relationship is the culmination of the ending of the past ones. Had those not ended, I would never be in this one.

There are two ways to look at moving forward from the loss of a relationship. One is the standard model: let it go and move on. The second, which I believe is more effective though less popular, is 'let it be and move forward.' When you have to let go of something, it implies that you were holding on to it in the first place. When you let it be, however, you're simply allowing things to exist as they are without the need for control or resistance.

Similarly, when you move on from something, you were meant to go back to that moment and move on from it. Whereas, when you move forward from something or someone, you are simply moving ahead, leaving everything behind as it was—a sense of acceptance. There is no need to erase the past. There is only a need to move forward from the past into a present which ultimately takes you to a future of your own.

It is important to know that no matter how much you force something, you cannot force what is not meant for you and similarly you cannot fight what is meant for you. In other words, you cannot fuck up what is meant for you. So trusting in this concept will bring a sense of peace.

In many ways, one must understand that rejection is merely redirection. And processing the pain of any rejection will empower you to redirect yourself onto a path that is meant for you.

When you said no, it broke my heart.
To become strangers now on paths apart.
What I did not know was that you gave me direction.
By letting me move forward with my fate's intention.
You said goodbye only to show me the light.
To the one I needed to meet who now was in sight.

Case Study 4
Sia's Story – The Quiet Hurt of Being Overlooked

Introduction

Sia was six years old when her light began to dim. She had once been a girl full of laughter and wonder, the kind whose joy could brighten any room. But by the time I met her, that joy had become rare. Her shoulders seemed to carry a weight too heavy for someone so young. Her eyes no longer searched the world with curiosity. Instead, they held something quieter, something sad.

She lived with her mother, Sheetal, and her older brother, Arjun. Their apartment was modest, tucked into a part of the city where people kept their struggles quiet. On the outside, Sheetal seemed like a woman who had it all together. She was admired for her style and poise. People often said she was graceful and warm. But behind closed doors, that warmth faded. What Sia experienced at home was very different from what others saw.

Sheetal gave her attention almost entirely to Arjun. He was the golden child, always praised, always seen. When he spoke, people listened. When he achieved even something small, it was celebrated. Sia, on the other hand, became the one blamed for everything that went wrong. She was the scapegoat.

If Sia accidentally spilled her milk at breakfast, her mother would snap, saying she was clumsy and asking why she could not be more like her brother. If Sia brought home a drawing from school, hopeful and proud, her mother would glance at it coldly and say it was messy and that Arjun could do better. These moments repeated themselves day after day. Over time, Sia stopped trying to be noticed. She began to believe she did not deserve to be noticed at all.

Even her birthdays were quiet. Her small achievements were ignored. She learned to expect nothing from home but silence or criticism. And though no one laid a hand on her, the emotional wounds were deep. Sia began to believe she was broken. That she was hard to love. That she was simply not enough.

When The Silence Spoke Too Loudly

One afternoon at school, Sia was sitting alone on the playground. She was not playing with the other children. She was just sitting still, staring at the ground. Her teacher, Ms Kapoor, noticed the change. She knelt beside her and asked gently if anything was wrong. Sia hesitated. Then she whispered something small but powerful.

She said, *'I am just bad. My mom says so.'*

Those words were enough to send a ripple through the school staff. Ms Kapoor referred her to the school counsellor, who soon realised this was more than sadness. This was a child living in emotional pain. After several conversations, the counsellor reached out to Sia's father. He agreed, though cautiously, to support therapy.

Creating a Safe Space for Healing

Sia came to therapy with quiet eyes and guarded movements. She needed more than a plan. She needed safety. She needed kindness and asked for nothing in return. We began slowly, with simple games and gentle words. Through play and drawing, she started to share her world in small pieces.

The First Step Was Trust

At first, I followed Sia's lead. If she wanted to paint, we painted. If she wanted to build with blocks, we did that too. Each time she tried something, I praised her gently, not for being perfect but for being present. In those early sessions, the goal was not to fix anything. It was to give her space to simply be. Slowly, she began to tell me about home. About how her mother spoke to her. About how she felt invisible. About how it felt to always come second.

Changing the Story She Believed

Sia believed she was not good enough. That belief had settled deep inside her. So we began to challenge it through stories and metaphors. We made up a tale about a small bird who was told it would never fly. But over time, the bird discovered it had strong wings and could soar higher than anyone expected. This was not just a story. It was Sia's way of beginning to imagine a different version of herself. One that was strong. One that mattered.

Helping Sia Understand Her Feelings

We also worked on emotional tools. I taught her how to breathe deeply when her feelings got too big. We made a feelings jar together, adding a bead each day to show how she felt. Red for anger, Blue for sadness and Yellow for happiness. This simple act helped her name her emotions and see that every feeling was valid.

Healing Beyond The Therapy Room

Sia's healing also needed support from her family. Her mother refused to join us in therapy. She said there was nothing wrong with her parenting. But Sia's father began to show more interest. In our sessions, I explained the idea of scapegoating and how damaging it can be. I helped him understand how his silence had allowed these patterns to continue.

He began to step in more often at home. He started to notice when Sheetal's words were too sharp. He began to spend time alone with Sia, asking about her day, praising her efforts, reminding her that she was loved. These small shifts mattered. They gave Sia a different kind of mirror. One that reflected her true self back to her with kindness.

A Brighter Story Begins

It did not happen all at once. But Sia began to change. Her drawings became more colourful, more confident. She stopped asking if her ideas were good. She started sharing them with pride. She began to speak up in class. She even made a few new friends. The girl who once whispered that she was bad, started to say things like, *I like how I drew this* or *I helped someone today.*

Her journey is not finished. The wounds from her mother's treatment will take time to fade. But Sia is no longer living in silence. She is learning to speak her truth. To believe in her worth. She is learning to soar, just like the little bird she created in her story.

Sia's Treatment Path

Therapy Goals:
- Rebuild Sia's self-esteem and help her let go of harmful beliefs

- Teach simple ways to manage emotions and feel safe in her body
- Strengthen relationships that help her feel secure and supported therapeutic interventions
- Play therapy to allow safe expression
- Storytelling to introduce new beliefs and build inner strength
- Gentle reframing to shift the way she saw herself

Parental Support:
- Educate her father about scapegoating and emotional harm
- Encourage consistent, loving presence in Sia's daily life

Long-term Support:
- Ongoing therapy to build confidence
- Consider group work or mentorship to offer healthy peer support

> **For You, the Reader**
>
> Sia's story may feel familiar to many. Perhaps you were once the child who felt overlooked. Or maybe you knew someone like Sia and did not have the words to name what was happening. Scapegoating is not always loud. It can be quiet, subtle and deeply damaging. It often hides in families that look perfect from the outside.
>
> But there is hope in the truth.
>
> When we begin to see the child behind the silence, when we offer safe places and kind words, healing becomes possible. Sia's journey is proof that the story we are given as children does not have to be the story we carry forever.
>
> If you have ever felt like the problem in your family.
>
> If you have questioned your worth.
>
> If you have been waiting to be seen.

Let Sia remind you: healing begins the moment someone truly sees you.

> You were never too much.
> You were never not enough.
> You were simply waiting to remember your own worth.

Episode 8
Why Don't You Love Me As I Love You?

She became ...
Not for the sake of a man
For the love of herself

As I said, I feel deeply. So when it comes to love, I love deeply as well. When you give yourself to someone with all your energy, all your being and everything you have to offer, you are shattered when they do not love you back the same way. And this was the story of my life.

I love unconditionally. Now, when I say this, I mean it. Love is unconditional, but relationships are not. And this was the ultimate learning lesson that life taught me. But before I begin the conversation on that aspect, let me digress to the moments that led to the torment of relationships that were hard to forget.

My relationships were real and they were long. They lasted, each more than a year and some even multiple years. In fact, it would be true to say that since the age of 14, I have never been single. Many people stay in the relationship out of factors that aren't substantial enough to rationalise being together. This was the plight of many of my past relationships, but mostly my final one before I met my life partner. I had been in a long-term relationship which, in my view, was happy, stable and full of promise. I genuinely believed we shared a common vision for the future. What I didn't realise, however, was that my partner had a different perspective on where the relationship was headed. While some circumstances may have been beyond our control, what was most difficult to accept was the lack of transparency. In the end, the decision was made unilaterally and quietly, without giving me the opportunity to understand or prepare.

The relationship ended in a way a screen play of Hollywood would enact. It should have been titled *The Missing, The Disappearance* or *The Vanishing*. To say I was humiliated would be an understatement. I was misled, I was betrayed and rejected—I felt failure at its deepest level.

I had loved with all my heart, body and mind—so why couldn't I be loved back in the same way? Why was I used, abused and led to believe we would be together, when the decision to move on had already been made? I was simply the last to know—actually, I was never told.

When someone vanishes on you without any indication, leaving no trace, you go through multiple stages of emotion. First, of course, comes worry and paranoia—wondering if something terrible has happened to the human being. Next comes disillusionment, where you begin to think thoughts that make no sense, such *as Would he actually leave me this way without any word, after so many years of love and courtship?* Then comes the hardest part—acceptance of a betrayal so intense that it could break anyone down and that is what happened to me.

I could not believe that my partner did not dignify me

enough to respectfully end our relationship with communication, with words, with actions and deem the rightful closure that any trustworthy relationship deserves. Rather, he just disappeared.

This was the final blow to my inner essence. Not only was I unable to accept that I was lovable, I now had lost all sense of self-worth, self-respect and self-esteem. And most of all, I had lost the faith in myself to create and manifest *true* love for me from another. I was not meant for true love, at least not in this lifetime.

This is where the impact of loss without closure intensifies into becoming a deep-rooted part of our own self. The internalisation of relationship failure can seep into the heart and mind quickly and transition into a sense of self-dismay.

An open-ended ending—torturous and painful to the point of feeling helpless and vulnerable; vulnerable not only to the situation but also to your own mind. You begin to spiral into an abyss of self-damage, furthering the illusion of a painful loss into something tangible—a loss caused by you, for there is no other reason, for there is no explanation. No one to speak with. No one to help you heal. You are your only answer, and now you physically are weak with a constant state of weakness—devastated and debilitated. Emotionally, you are drained and sensationally, you are suffering.

I would rather have had him not love me, not care for me, then to do what was done to me.

> *Love me not if you cannot love me with grace and love me not if you cannot bestow respect and dignity to me.*

This is why I say: love can be unconditional but relationships are not. It is important to understand the distinction, to love without condition does not mean to devalue, to disrespect or to negate your feelings from the equation. Do not allow yourself to reach a point where someone can actually treat you in the way I was treated. It is true when they say, 'What you allow is what will happen.' I allowed my partner to think it is okay to disappear and vanish without a trace and not allot me the basic decency to end our relationship face to face. I let that happen and the damage it did to me was unfathomable. I had lost all trust, not only in love, not only in humanity, but also in my ability and myself. Beyond that, a level of insecurity and fear of abandonment set so deep into my system that I would say I was unable to live with any secure feeling for decades after.

The most basic need of the soul is to experience unconditional love; more so, unconditional acceptance. But what the journey is meant to teach you is that the unconditional love and acceptance comes from within you. If I could speak to my 18-year-old self, I would ensure that she knew what we imagine love to be is actually an aspiration for acceptance. It's the inner want that we seek so strongly that we lose sight of true love. We allow ourselves to be taken for granted under the guise of unconditional love.

What is this 'unconditional love'?

Everyone has their own definitions and connotations, but for me, unconditional love is total acceptance—of them and of you. The aspect of 'you' being the most important in the journey of love is one that you should never forget. Once you love yourself, you will be able to seek out what is meant. It is a painful ride, but it will lead you to peace.

You will find that true love is inner love and you will appreciate it as much as it holistically appreciates you. But before you find it, you will experience pain, undergo heartbreak, feel betrayal and will be hurt. Just remember to keep the boundary of self-regard strong and high, for through this journey, you mustn't forsake.

This level of disregard for the self does not only apply to relationships that are romantic, but rather to relationships in general throughout life. The desire to please regardless of condition or at the expense of the self is intrinsically a human coping mechanism.

Many of us become a version of who we are not because we are scared of losing people. What we do not realise is that in this journey of being a version of you that is not authentic, you inadvertently lose a part of yourself. We do this out of fear when we try to be someone else rather than being our true selves.

Why do we do this? Especially when we know that we are losing who we actually are and slowly living a life that is not even ours, but rather a life determined by the people around us. Our choices and decisions are often based on what makes them happy, rather than what makes us happy. Our beliefs and value systems begin to shift—becoming more pathological and shaped by society, rather than grounded in our individuality. This is all because we are scared of ending up alone and losing those around us.

What if I told you that most relationships based on being the public self as we discussed earlier will eventually end? What if I told you that these relationships are time limited?

When we are unable to become our real self, we will never be able to become our ideal selves. And this aspect is only going to lead to thoughts and actions which are contradicting to the life we are meant to live.

Live your own life. If you keep trying to do what others want, if you keep trying to think the way others think, you'll end up living someone else's life. Be you. Live as you. Think like you. Believe as you. Only then will you learn to love yourself—as you, for you, by you.

Episode 9
Reflections Taught By Wounds

Beauty is the beast making you it's prey, if you succumb to the game,
you will forever play
Shine from within, not to alter the reality,
Love you as is, forced beauty is brutality

I was not only in a space of mental let down when it came to loving myself, but also unable to accept who I was physically. As an early bloomer, my breasts were full to bosom, my body was voluptuous and simultaneously I was surrounded by skinny, lean-bodied teenage girls. This made me feel fat. In every aspect of the element, I began body shaming myself. I was not happy with any part of my body and my inner angst increased my cravings for sugar. This triggered desire for eating food to feel better and binge eating—an I would binge to replace any sorrow and compensate for any void.

I would eat and I would throw up. I would place first two, then three, then four fingers, as my bulimia worsened through the years. Bulimia wasn't a disorder alone for me, it became a coping mechanism and that is what made it deadlier than the disorder itself. It became my escape—from pain, from trauma, from sadness and eventually from anything.

I ended up in the hospital a few times, but the scars of that chronic eating disorder remain with me even today. From hair loss issues to metabolic disorders, the bingeing of food to purging has developed into autoimmune disorders which require lifelong therapy. You could effectively say that 'I threw (up) my life away.'

If I could only talk to my sixteen-year-old self, I would explain to her that you should respect and love your body for what it is. What you think is fat is actually voluptuously sexy. What you think is big is beautiful and attractive. What you see as different is, in truth, your uniqueness—it's what makes you, *you*. You should love yourself. You should never shame yourself. And you should never harm yourself.

Life lessons come in unique forms. Most of the time, they come through painful situations. I am yet to fully understand the correlation between struggle and growth—the way life uses it to help us evolve. But I do accept today that it is a phenomenon that exists to make us better human beings.

When we focus on lessons, especially those that come in the form of tough love through life, we realise that there must be some reason. The cliché quote is that everything happens for a reason. However, what if I said that everything does not happen for a reason, but rather happens to prevent something worse. You may be wondering why I'm talking about this at this point within the book which is actually focusing on body dysmorphia. The reason is because here is where I want to create the distinction between reflection and rumination. When you become hyper-focused on a part of your body or a perceived flaw, it often stems from constant rumination. These obsessive thoughts can lead to destructive behaviours and compulsions.

Had I reflected on my weight issues—the fact that I was more voluptuous than those around me, I would have been able to see things from an external point of view rather than an internal one. In other words, I would externalise it and reflect on how I was feeling and seek more effective and less destructive methods of resolution to what I was feeling.

The constant ruminating made me internalise all of the negative thought processes that my brain was feeding me and led to impulsivity in terms of wanting to resolve this feeling with immediate gratification. Reflection and rumination are both one and the same in terms of where they stem from. Both are intense in nature and focus on the reason. The only difference is that reflection allows us to look into the '*why*', whereas rumination focuses intensely on the '*how*'. When we do not have an understanding of why and only focus on how, we are then pulled into a vicious cycle of thought patterns that fuel fear and lead to a mental breakdown.

Reflection allows us to know what is happening in order to prevent something worse from happening, whereas rumination just makes us feel that what we are going through is permanent and, therefore, there is no reprieve. When you ruminate, your thoughts actually become things—things that seem factual to you. When you are facing any form of obsessive thinking patterns regarding a part of you or your life, it is important to journal and reflect on what you are going through. This will enable you to understand the source of the pain and know that your thoughts in general are not facts, but rather assumptions.

Case Study 5
Aarav – Living in the Shadow of Fear and Cultural Silence

Client Profile
- Name: Aarav (pseudonym)
- Age: 31
- Background: Indian heritage, second-generation immigrant
- Presenting Concerns: Emotional instability, chronic anxiety, low self-worth, relationship difficulties, disconnection from self

Early Environment And Family Dynamics
Aarav grew up in a household marked by rigid discipline, strict rules and constant supervision. His parents, deeply committed to cultural traditions, believed that control was necessary for raising a respectable, morally upright child. Every action, choice and emotion was scrutinised through the lens of community judgement and family honour.

Disobedience, even minor, was met with punishment—physical or emotional. Though the physical discipline was not always extreme, it was consistent enough to instil deep-seated fear. More impactful, however, was the emotional environment:

cold, rule-bound and devoid of space for self-expression. Emotional needs were dismissed, vulnerability was discouraged and compliance was equated with love and acceptance.

From an early age, Aarav was conditioned to suppress his emotions and needs in order to maintain peace and earn approval. He was told what to feel, who to be and how to behave, all under the guise of respect, obedience and family pride. Love often felt conditional. Failure wasn't just personal—it was portrayed as a disgrace to the entire family.

Cultural Stigma Around Mental Health
One of the most significant barriers to Aarav's healing was the cultural narrative around mental health, particularly for men. Therapy was seen not just as unnecessary, but shameful—something for the weak or broken. As a boy, he was taught that strength meant silence and endurance. Any emotional expression, especially sadness or vulnerability, was framed as weakness.

By the time Aarav began considering therapy, he had already internalised these beliefs. He struggled to justify his need for support, fearing he would dishonour his family or appear ungrateful. For years, he battled his symptoms alone, believing his distress was a personal failure rather than a reflection of deep emotional wounding.

Emotional And Psychological Impact
The long-term effects of Aarav's upbringing became evident in nearly every area of his adult life:
- **Emotional Instability:** Aarav often found himself overwhelmed by feelings he couldn't name. He was either emotionally numb or flooded—rarely in balance. He struggled to manage frustration, sadness, and especially guilt.

- **Fear-Based Living:** Even in adulthood, his decisions were dictated more by fear than desire. Fear of judgement, failure and rejection followed him into work, friendships and romantic relationships.
- **Attachment and Trust Issues:** Aarav feared closeness but also feared being alone. In relationships, he often over-accommodated or withdrew, expecting criticism or abandonment.
- **Lack of Self-Identity:** Years of suppressing his preferences and opinions left him unsure of who he really was. His self-worth was entirely shaped by others' approval.
- **Daily Dysfunction:** Basic routines felt overwhelming. His body carried years of stress—manifesting in fatigue, insomnia, difficulty concentrating and chronic tension.

The Therapeutic Journey

Aarav's healing began slowly, first by challenging the belief that therapy was a betrayal of his culture or masculinity. Creating a safe, non-judgemental space was essential. Therapy focused on:

- Understanding the impact of emotional suppression and its roots in family dynamics.
- Validating his pain and helping him let go of the narrative that he was 'too sensitive' or 'not good enough'.
- Teaching nervous system regulation, such as grounding and breathwork, to help reduce emotional flooding.
- Exploring boundaries, both emotional and physical, which had never been allowed growing up.
- Reclaiming his identity, through values work, inner child healing and journaling practices.
- Developing self-compassion, which helped him grieve the childhood he never got and reconnect with his authentic self.

Over time, Aarav began to notice a shift. He was able to pause before reacting, to speak his truth without overwhelming guilt and to see himself not as broken, but as someone who had survived with strength.

> **For you, the Reader**
> 1. **Cultural Discipline Can Mask Emotional Abuse:**
>   What is considered normal or necessary in one culture may deeply wound a child's sense of self. It's essential to assess parenting practices through the lens of emotional development—not just cultural norms.
> 2. **Mental Health Stigma Is Gendered And Cultural:**
>   In many communities, especially for men, seeking therapy is viewed as weakness. Therapeutic engagement often begins with validating this belief system while gently offering new ways of understanding strength.
> 3. **Fear-Based Parenting Shapes The Nervous System:**
>   A child who grows up in fear learns to live in survival mode. Without intervention, this shows up later as anxiety, reactivity, emotional shutdown or chronic dysregulation.
> 4. **Healing Requires Reclaiming The Right To Feel:**
>   Suppressed emotions don't disappear—they become symptoms. The work of therapy often begins by helping clients feel safe enough to feel at all.
> 5. **Culturally Sensitive Care Must Balance Respect With Truth:**
>   Healing doesn't mean rejecting one's culture. It means learning to separate identity from inherited pain and giving oneself permission to live freely and fully.

This case is a reminder that trauma isn't always loud. Sometimes it's woven into the rules we're told to follow, the silence we're taught to keep and the love we're taught we must earn. But healing is always possible—especially when someone is finally given the space to choose themselves.

Episode 10
Why Did You Leave So Soon ?

My father—my first love, my hero, my guide, my oxygen, my lifeline, my best friend, my heart, my soul, my beats—my everything.

I am sure there are many people in the world that feel the same. My father was the only man who accepted me with all my flaws, who taught me the meaning of unconditional love, whose love and affection knew no bounds and who sacrificed everything to ensure his family was well taken care of. But these were the happy moments, with such exuberance comes pain—for life is made up of a balance of sentiment.

My father met with a near fatal car accident in 1979. He was pronounced clinically dead for two minutes, only to resurface with critical injuries to his eyes and his bodily system. After numerous surgeries, nine to be exact, my father did manage to find stability in health and lead a life with double vision. From wearing a patch to eventually adjusting to eyesight issues, Daddy (Poppy as I affectionately called him) went back to being the life of the party.

Through the years after, I have seen my dad struggle,

recovering from the accident to face cardiac issues, diabetes, hypertension and eventually a quintuple bypass. Yet, his love never hindered, his attitude remained as it always was and he never allowed any of his problems to become a burden on any of us. I remember the year 1990, when I went into the ICU to see him after the bypass surgery; he could not speak, but he took my hand, and with his index finger he etched the words, *'I heart U'* on my palm. That was my Poppy, no matter how much pain he would have been feeling at that time, no matter what level of angst he may be going through, he never ignored any opportunity to tell me he loved me. That was my father—the one man who gave me more happiness in one moment than anyone could give me in a lifetime.

When my father passed away, it was the only time I decided to seek therapy and spend two hours a week communicating with a professional to release my inner pain. My father did not just pass away from illness or with sudden death; rather, his life ended because of medical misjudgement and unfortunately lack of professional medical healthcare.

I remember carrying my father's ashes with me in my lap as I flew back from New Jersey to Delhi. His ashes were to be immersed in the holy Ganges River in Haridwar where all of his family members and my ancestors' rites were performed.

I was numb. I was also alone. My mother and my sister had to take care of the arrangements required in America and, therefore, this journey was one that I had to take by myself. With my father's spiritual guide alongside me, we travelled to Haridwar to complete all the rites and rituals according to our religion. Generally, only a son can perform these rites and I was questioned by the holy men in the temples, only to react with the deepest of glares and a fire within, stating I am his daughter, I am his son, I am all of it and I will perform each rite in this capacity.

From the ashes to the *pujas* (the rituals we perform for the soul to rest in peace) each moment took me deeper into regret as I had unfortunately been arguing with my father for four months prior to his death. I had travelled to America from my base in Mumbai and was fortunate to spend the entire week with him leading up to the fatal surgery. We had been in regular contact for months before that, but I had been carrying some negativity due to disagreements we had over certain life decisions. Daily calls became weekly calls and in his heart, he knew I was upset with him. This aspect finally shattered me. I had so much I wanted to say—words unspoken, explanations I needed to give my dad, reasons to describe what was going on in my mind and my life, but he was not there anymore. I could not speak to him anymore, I could not tell him how stupid I was to hold onto the disappointment. I could not tell him I was sorry for having an ego. I could not do anything for he was not going to be able to listen to me anymore. My father was gone. And I was left behind with guilt, with sadness and with pain.

Life can sometimes be a tough crowd. Do not leave things unsaid, do not hold onto grudges, do not allow resentment to build to the point of detaching from those you love. If I could have one moment to tell my father anything, it would be that we may disagree; we may not see eye to eye, but there is no one and nothing that could ever create a gap between us. It is okay to agree to disagree; what we need to understand is that we must agree to disagree with love.

I allowed ego and immaturity to take precious moments of time and conversation with my father because I never imagined he would not be there again. It took me a long time to forgive myself and though I may have today, I know there is a part of me that is scarred and may never heal.

When we lose a loved one, there is no greater pain. I remember being asked if the pain lessens, if it ever gets any better. And as much as it hurts to hear this, the truth is that it does not stop hurting. In fact, the pain does not go away—it just becomes bearable. We begin to cope with the loss.

We are not meant to forget the loss; we just feel the loss a little less. Losing someone that we have loved hurts on multiple levels, not because we were used to that individual, habituated to their presence, but we were attached to their energies. Our soul was attached to their soul—this is where the pain stems from—the inability to feel them, to see them, to hear them. All that remains is a gaping void and silence.

The reason why I'm explaining this phenomenon is because it is important to understand that just because we are unable to see, feel or hear our loved ones, it does not mean that we cannot move forward with them. I move forward with my father in my mind, heart and soul every day. I sense him with me even though I cannot see him, hear him or touch him. This is how we can overcome the loss that our senses are feeling and enable the pain to become bearable.

The five stages of grief were actually created for individuals that were given a diagnosis that was terminal. These stages, though very helpful to many are not necessarily meant to be the only way to grieve the loss of a loved one. You do not have to process grief as society expects you to. You must process your own grief in whichever way your system and yourself feel comfortable. If, for you, healing means choosing to celebrate in order to overcome the loss, or surrounding yourself with people who uplift and celebrate life—that's okay, too. Please don't burden yourself with guilt or shame if your grief doesn't look like constant sadness or isolation. Grieving doesn't have to mean shutting yourself off from the world. When you lose a loved one and are grieving their loss, you are not meant to lose yourself in the process. This only leads to exacerbated negativity and intense feelings of loneliness.

Loving yourself through the process of grief is the most beautiful thing you can do for yourself and for your loved one.

When I said goodbye my smile was taken.
You left my side asleep not to awaken.
As your face appeared in my dreams I knew to be true.
Your presence was stripped but in absence I still feel you.

Episode 11
Love That Led Me Back To Myself

The three words which matter the most, the three words I always wanted to hear. The three words that would rule the first four decades of my life—I LOVE YOU. The need (yes I was addicted to this) to be loved was something so important to me that every action committed was as a result of a desire for this reaction.

According to research, when you are ignored, or not given attention from the one whom you crave it the most, your brain releases a sensation in your system which is equivalent to physical pain. That is why when your heart breaks, you as an individual feel a sincere ache in your body. A lump develops in your throat, your stomach begins to churn, your eyes swell up with tears, your heart starts to race and your body begins to shut down. Symptoms similar to disease and illness begin to manifest within your insides.

And why?

Because someone ignored you. Reading that now, it might make you question your own intelligence. But the truth is this: you weren't dumb—you were human.

***

As human beings, we give too much importance to those around us. And we tend to give less importance to ourselves. Our emotions are controlled by external forces, by beings that may or may not even hold any significance in our lives. But at that moment, they do. We are affected by what they say, what they do and most importantly, what they DON'T say or do. They say the key to happiness is a bad memory and hearing loss. So basically, as human beings, we would rather be senile and deaf than actually prohibit our emotions from controlling us. We, the supposed 'most intelligent' species on the planet, lose daily to the battle with emotions. When we will be able to say '*I have emotions, but my emotions don't have me,*' only then will we be able to live happily.

This was my life. An emotional, controlled roller coaster ride, which at times felt like a free fall, and at others, like I was going in circles, upside down, in 90 degree angle curves. Without love, I lost my sense of worth. Without worth, I lost my sense of self. And without a self, I simply faded—I no longer existed. Imagine feeling all this because someone didn't like you. When you walk into a room and wonder who likes you, I can tell you today after everything I have experienced, that you are yet naïve and young. But the day you walk into a room and wonder who you actually like, pat yourself on the back for you have grown.

The journey has been challenging, filled with multiple meltdowns, a lot of self-persecution, doubt, disappointment, pain and suffering. As I reflect, I can say these experiences made me who I am today.

Those words still matter. They do. And always will.

But now, the three words, 'I love you', have a completely new meaning for me. What I didn't know then was that the love I craved the most wasn't from anyone else—it was from me.

It took me time, I still remember how my heart would ache each time I didn't get the validation I desired. I could not understand how one person can be dismissed so easily by those that she has done so much for. Unconditional love for me came easily, but it just never came easily when I had to love myself. If I had to list down 5 things I loved the most, I would never consider naming myself (an exercise I use to mentor teens today). Your name should be on the top of the list, ideally. This is not selfish; it is, in fact, quite the opposite. If you can love yourself, you will be more selfless towards those around you, as you will be in a happier state of mind. The level of angst one carries when they are unhappy with who they are resonates to catastrophic levels.

Loving yourself is a process—it is actively putting your energy towards creating change. Change within yourself, and in the way you view yourself and most importantly changing your thought processes. The first step I took was to write down what I genuinely appreciated about myself. I still remember being asked, during my time as a contestant in the Miss India USA pageant, what I considered to be my greatest asset. Without hesitation, I answered, 'My heart.' Because my heart knew love—it knew how to give it freely and it loved without judgement or discrimination. That, I realised, was my true strength.

Today, I still feel the same, but what do you do when your heart has been broken so many times? Just like a consistent fracture to the same bone causes weakness, heartbreaks led to my heart becoming fragile. So I decided to take charge of resurrecting the strength within me. I listed all the facets within me that I knew were valuable. Slowly, I realised the validation I could give myself was enough. I no longer needed to seek recognition from anyone else. My purpose in life was simply to become the best human being I could be—to grow a little more each day. And that journey had nothing to do with anyone else.

When you start to see yourself through altered eyes, trust me when I say that you will see something beautiful. I started to smile as I looked in the mirror.

Instinctively, my face would glow as my mind wandered to moments of me as a mom, as a daughter, as a person; *in any role, as anyone*. There was so much to love about me and this new love knew no bounds.

When you love yourself, you give others a reason to love you as I said in the past many times. In the same way, you advocate or promote causes, products or services to others because you care for them—when you truly love yourself, you enable others to love you as well. But loving yourself is not the same as accepting yourself, nor is it the same as self-awareness. Loving yourself means offering *unconditional love* to who you are, even for the parts you may not necessarily like.

If I was to ask you to name five people that you love, you would most likely say your family members, your pets or maybe even your best friends. You rarely would say yourself. When in actuality, the first person on the list should be you followed by your loved ones. This creates a sense of authenticity, where you genuinely relate to those around you as yourself, not as the pretence of who you think they would love. By default, it allows you to feel validated and loved for who you are, rather than for who you are not. Once your thought patterns and behavioural patterns are in sync with this sentiment, you will begin to feel safe within the relationship that you have with yourself. This relationship will be the most important relationship of your life.

Episode 12
I Know You Love My Body But Do You Love Me?

Lucky is the man who sips from her potion
From her womb births a fire
Of passion, lust and desire

When you believe in your heart that no one can love you, you succumb to distorted thoughts plagued with negativity. When you have faced abuse—even sexual assault—you begin to view yourself with very different eyes.

This was my story. As much as passion dominated many of my relationships, the one commitment I made in marriage needed more than just passion. In my mind, sex was important but as I had children and the years went by, I expected love to be shown in different ways as well. I wanted to be surprised, I wanted to be courted, I wanted to be loved in other ways—basically I suddenly wanted my partner to be someone he was not. This was not a fair ask, I understand now.

One of the biggest issues I see in relationships today and have faced myself, is the aspect of sex and intimacy and its implications in a relationship. Keeping physical intimacy consistent and the challenges that come with it, is one aspect of the relationship which transitions through many phases. It is also one of the most common reasons why relationships crumble.

From the honeymoon period, when couples can't keep their hands off each other, to later years, many admit that their relationships dissolved not only due to a lack of physical intimacy but, more importantly, a lack of effort. Now there could be a host of valid reasons for this to happen, notably justifiable on both sides—such as pregnancy, having children, job requirements, health and exhaustion as well.

I was inundated with multiple responsibilities and sex—which is very important to me—got pushed lower on the list. I was either exhausted or just not interested. I have always found my partner to be highly attractive and a fabulous lover, but my needs just reduced and with it the want to indulge became less.

At this point, the relationship goes through a real test. When a woman is sexually rejected, she begins to feel physically invalidated. She feels she is not attractive enough. Her body is not sexual or desirable and she begins to notably retreat and alienate herself from being proactive in initiating sexual intimacy. When a man is sexually rejected, he feels emotionally invalidated. He begins to feel emasculated and his thoughts spiral into a rabbit hole: that he is not a satisfactory lover, that he may be unable to perform and soon he begins to suffer from performance anxiety as well.

However justified this may be, when sex is perceived by most people as an 'effort' or a 'task' rather than a communication of love, inconsistency inevitably creates negativity on both sides. And that's what happens with many couples. She says his desire became an annoyance to her—a disregard for what she wanted, a lack of love for her well-being and an absence of care for how she felt at the time. Before long, it turned into a chore, a task she undertook merely to fulfil what she saw as a marital duty. Suddenly, sex was no longer pleasurable; it had become a nuisance. Rather than seeing sex as a love language, one sees it as a language of control.

It takes time to realise that the desire being shown was, in fact, your partner's way of expressing his love. It was his love language.

Starting to view basic acts of love in this manner helps tremendously to recognise love in its decoded form. You begin to appreciate this measure as your partner's method of love. It also helps to cultivate reciprocation within yourself. Just as we naturally respond in the language spoken by a loved one, this too is a response in the love language your partner uses—an unspoken desire for you to speak it back.

Emotional wellness depends on the physical wellness of the relationship and this aspect is connected to the mental comprehension of what the act of love truly means.

I often hear couples say, *'Both my partner and I love each other, so where are we going wrong? Why are we unable to understand one another?'* and this is where I say both you and your partner do love one another but you are speaking your love in two seemingly different dialects. And, therefore, you are unable to understand that you are saying I love you to one another.

We spend so much of our time shutting our partners down that we truly do not allow them to tell us or show us their love in their way. In many ways, we rarely get to know our partners in their full depth, as most of our conversations revolve around asking them to think like us, speak like us and essentially be like us—rather than allowing them the space to be themselves.

It is imperative that both partners understand what is important to each one of them, but not so much in the form of a need—rather as a way of how they convey their love for one another. If being physical is your partner's way of expression, do the same back with an equal quotient.

If your partner's love language is to spend a lot of time planning a birthday, buying or making a special gift, surprising you with things—acknowledge this love dialect and speak to your partner back in this way. Even though you now view these things as frivolous or insignificant, this indulgence enables a validation of love with a similar form of giving back. This is your journey towards adapting to each other's lingo of love.

Episode 13
All This Love, Left Unreturned

Love is not in your control. Nothing is in your control. Even controlling your own emotions and reactions are technically not in your control. You aim to achieve this point of nirvana and aspire to become the epitome of self-control, but that thought process is, in itself, a fallacy. Please don't set unrealistic expectations for yourself by stating you will never react to any given situation, for this element in itself is setting you up for disappointment. The objective of love is decrypting it to understanding that it is made up of a plethora of mixed traits wherein conflict and forgiveness are part and parcel of the life of love. The minute you detach to the point of indifference, love ceases to exist in its actual form.

Today, as I reflect upon the relationships of my past, I can truly say I am as much to blame for their failure as my partner at the time. I was so dominated by the perception of love having to be only a glorious state of mind, that any negativity would spiral me into a condition of doom. Relationships can become bipolar if you allow them to. That is when the state of affairs are at the two extremes: manic euphoria and manic angst. This is the final phase. You get so caught up in trying to create magic, that you forget to realise magic is not created, it is experienced.

The truth was that I was so busy trying to create it every day—crafting joy-filled moments with love bursting at the seams—that I was too exhausted to notice the relationship had already ended. This was not love.

This was ego. I had to win. With each relationship, I could not lose. If I lost, I failed. If I failed, I was not important. If I was not important, I was not loved. How could I not be loved? How could he not love me? It suddenly became all about me. I know my heart is and has always been capable of an abundance of love, but the thought of rejection manifested a side of me that I myself could not recognise.

Why?

The ego; it is the part of your mind that connects your conscious being to your subconscious, thus distinguishing you from the self of the other. When you distinguish yourself from another, you are automatically giving yourself a sense of self-importance. This, in itself, is the opposite of love.

From the ego also stems the self. Not being able to free yourself from the self can be deeply detrimental to your relationships. Not to be confused with detachment, which could be labelled indifference, freedom of the self is liberation from being affected when triggered. We all have fear within us. In a relationship, the main element of reaction is based upon the nature of being afraid. Aside from physical fears, humans have deep-rooted psychological fears within the recesses of their brain as well. If we are able to liberate the self from the fear of being hurt, rejected, harmed, ignored, insulted and mainly not loved back, these elements may not affect us as intensely and subjectively as they do.

Perception of the trigger is a reality that our brain processes based upon our assessment of the trigger. If we automatically assume it to be personal, it becomes distinctively just that. As human beings, there is the defence mechanism of fight or flight syndrome embedded within each of us. This mechanism instantly appears when the mind and body feel attacked. Our heart begins to palpitate, mind starts to race, the gut gets agitated and nausea sets in. This can also be categorised as a panic attack. This syndrome is meant to protect us from harm, but when it manifests unconditionally and consistently, one can assume that it needs to be controlled.

The part of the fight-or-flight response that we often overlook—or remain unaware of—is the space in between: the freeze. This is the moment where we begin to feel stuck. When we are in touch with both the ego and the heart, we reach the point of choice—whether to react or to respond. Reaction comes from a state of mind; response comes from a state of heart. When I say heart instead of love, I am referring to the heart, I am not referring to the emotion of love. When we respond, we take into consideration the impact that the situation has on us, but also what the individual in front of us is possibly going through. In this particular instance, we are able to pause. Breathe for a moment and then decide whether or not to initiate a counter attack. When we are reacting on the other hand, there is no pause. There is no breath and there is only pure impulsivity.

My tendency to react had been one of the greatest weaknesses within my system. The impulse to defend myself immediately without any thought process filter caused more harm within the self than the trigger ever did. I would succumb to irrational and unreasonable behaviour, causing greater damage to not only the relationship, but also to all those involved. I found myself resorting to methods of counter attack which were problematic and baseless. The thing to consider here was the reason behind this method of conduct, it was the self; the self-conceit, the self-adulation, the self-arrogance and overall, the narcissism. Self-love is not to be confused with any of these traits. Though the ultimate goal is to love the self, true self-love means freeing ourselves from the negative elements that work against us.

None of us are immune to having an ego, it is about not allowing our ego to have us. There are many ways in which we can introduce a process of thinking where our ego becomes a source of guidance for us, but does not become a controlling factor within our behavioural patterns. Simply replacing expectations with requirements, in itself, alters the process of thinking to a great degree. Expectations come from the ego, whereas requirements come from the heart. Expectations are meant to make us feel better as individuals, while requirements are essential for the relationship and, therefore, make the relationship feel better.

I always tell my clients that when you come to seek advice from me as an individual, you are my client, but when you come to me as a couple, the relationship is my client. And here is where we look at our relationship and understand the importance of its role and its outcome. Distinguishing ego from heart begins with knowing the difference between wants and needs. When we shift our focus from wants to needs, the mind accepts that not all needs will be met—with that acceptance comes peace. We may be disheartened, but we do not impulsively act out with negativity. Saying 'I want' versus 'I need' impacts both the relationship and your partner. When you begin to see your partner's request as a genuine need—something essential—you become more proactive in fulfilling it.

Acceptance of your partner comes from a space of superiority, as we, as individuals, are not supposed to accept or deny our partners; we are supposed to accommodate them as the people that they are. Hence, when we acknowledge and accommodate our partners, we give them the recognition that they deserve as well as the validation to be who they are.

These thinking patterns take time to develop in relationships and they could be considered relational communication skill sets rather than just communication developmental skills. A key factor to note is what happens when a problem arises in a relationship: why are we so quick to fight each other rather than the problem itself? Is it because, as human beings, we instinctively make it about ourselves and view any problem as a personal attack?

What if I was to tell you that being less confrontational and being more conversational would lead to a better outcome and a more rational path to resolution? We join hands in relationships then why are we not able to join our minds in battling our issues?

Contradiction addressed through confrontation or through control, merely requires conversation and compromise. The moment we start to feel that we are sacrificing for one another, the relationship may already be at a point of potential loss. It is not about sacrifice, it is about compromise. This is where a relationship finds itself feeling safe.

When we say love is freedom from the self, it is the ability to compartmentalise your emotions wherein you are able to perceive the trigger as less of a personal attack and more of a mere circumstance. Circumstances by nature are less fear-filled and cause a lower impulse to react irrationally.

Episode 14
Even Love Has Storms

Love is an energy force. Like any frequency, it manifests at high rates over a period of time. Love can send waves and vibrations within the body. There is a euphoria that comes with being in love and when being loved. The body manifests sensations in abundance; continuous smiles, heartbeats that pound, butterflies in the tummy and a sudden superpower of being in total control. You suddenly have the key to happiness—LOVE.

Love, however, is encrypted. It is a code which many of us are yet to decrypt. The key you are holding onto requires you to understand it in order for you to use it normally. Love is not a bed of roses. It is made up of multiple attributes such as want, desire, appreciation, trust, respect and acceptance. But it is also made up of fear, selflessness, forgiveness, growth, healing and most importantly—freedom.

The first step to understanding love is decrypting it.

Love decrypted is freedom. Freedom from the ego, freedom from the self, freedom from possession, freedom from attachment, 'free' from any 'dom'-ination.

Relationships are hard. If you hear anyone say otherwise,

they are lying. Happily, 'relation-ed'—a term I coined—is a paradox. You can achieve happiness in relationships, but at no point are you happily relation-ed consistently. Today, if you come to me saying you are in a constant state of happiness or wish to be chronically positive, I would actually tell you that this is toxic in nature. One is not meant to feel happy all the time; such a state is considered a form of hyper-euphoria and it calls for further investigation.

If I knew this, I would have saved myself a lot of grief. I assumed (yes assuming is making an ass out of me and you, but tell that to an 18-year-old in 'love') I had to be happy. More than that, I had to make sure he was happy. I had to make sure each moment was special, each day was epic, each instant was bliss-filled where both of us had to have plastic smiles like Barbie and Ken and if it wasn't, well the apocalypse had arrived. It was the end of the world as I knew it.

> Truth number 1: You are not responsible for 'his or her' happiness.
> Truth number 2: Some days are gonna suck. And that's okay.
> Truth number 3: You are not Barbie & Ken.

Love is not meant to be a state of consistent contentment. If it is, then it isn't love. It is infatuation. Love is meant to evoke emotions and feelings within you that are both dark and light. If you don't feel hate, you haven't felt love. If you don't feel angst, you are not in love. The idea is to detach from being affected by these emotions, not by negating them in their totality. To feel is important, to control the reaction to that feeling is where the issue lies. Most of us fail to understand this aspect. The eighteen-year-old me would feel jealousy and anger and would act upon those, triggering me into a potential emotional meltdown.

When I was forty-plus, I realised that I have to feel jealousy and anger, for it indicates that I yet care, but I love enough to not break down into shambles. I have the freedom from my own impulse to not break, though I may not have total control over it.

The idea is to be non-attached. Non-attachment allows you to separate yourself from emotion—not by fully grasping or analysing it, but by allowing it to exist and pass through you, without leaving a lingering impact.

The greatest peace comes from knowing that what you are feeling—though negative in nature—is temporary yet necessary for a healthy relationship. Remember when I spoke about the three selves, it is imminent that the real self, the actual self, presents itself during the tenure of your relationship. It is this self which brings a truth to the bond that you both share. And it is this self, which will ultimately take you to the ideal self.

A moment of angst and my heart would fear
I didn't know this, did not mean the end was near
I fought to control, to make the bad into good
Not knowing the moment was meant to be understood
The fight was a blessing, disguised bliss,
The screams were not needed, if only just a hug and a kiss

Episode 15
Chained By What I Call Love

Holding onto things is a human characteristic we all possess. Whether it is good for us or not, we don't leave. We hold on until it becomes so destructive that it destroys everyone involved, including us. This applies to all bonds and connections, not just the romantic ones. It could be familial, friendship or courtship, but if the relationship is causing undue stress and angst, it really is better to walk away. And that was something I could never do.

Ideally when we think about the intricacies associated with attachment to a person, more so a living thing, it is not the person per say that we are attached to, but rather the experiences, the memories and the daily moments of togetherness. That being said, one cannot deny that the loss of a person creates a void. Yet it is important to remember that this void comes not from love itself, but from being accustomed to their presence and the routines you shared. Love itself holds no attachment—it's the routine, the familiarity that we become attached to. For me, no matter how 'bad' the relationship got, I chose to stay. The fear of missing out—FOMO—meant more to me than my own well-being. I clung not to the person, but to the idea of what I might lose. This again, is related to the aspect that I always assumed myself and my self-health to be of insignificance. In my mind, I deserved it, whatever was happening was something that I contributed to, so I just deserved it.

Walking away from a situation you are habituated to depends greatly on your ability to think clearly with applied logic and rationale. I did not possess logical reasoning; for me, everything was emotionally guided.

All my decisions, my thought processes, my reactions, whatever these may be, were steered by my heart. Clarity in thought gives you the ability to apply reason to why you are with this person, whether it is a friend, family or a lover and what makes it valuable. Thinking about yourself during this period does not make you selfish; it provides stability and balance for both partners, because the longer you stay in a relationship that is not viable, the more toxic it becomes. And with toxicity comes imbalance of health and spirit.

I had retained so many friendships and relationships that both my heart and mind knew were unhealthy for me. Yet I found myself unable to release myself from the equation. In the end, the bond did suffer a brutal end leading to a time when we never spoke to one another. A completion of this sort leaves you with a much more intense quotient of bitterness. All good moments of the past negate to the point of being reminders of all things negative. You can never look back and smile, and you will find yourself cringing at the thought of when you were together. This particular aspect I find to be sad. If I could go back, I would have distanced myself at an earlier stage with the communication and closure required at that point. This way, I could salvage some good feelings about the connection and move on towards the future with positivity rather than anger or regret.

Life teaches us many things. We need to learn to imbibe them earlier on, rather than after the act. I had always been a reactive learner, but eventually I learnt to be a proactive processor. I didn't want to be the same person that received the message after the damage was done. I would rather be the individual who pre-empts a situation to the point of educating myself prior to any eruption.

The most natural things often feel unnatural to us—which is why, as human beings, our instinct is to stay and fight, even when letting go might be the wiser path. Time and time again, we are presenting ourselves as warriors trying to hold onto and control the relationship with as much force as possible. Ironically, staying and fighting is unnatural, yet we convince ourselves it is the normal—and even the most natural—response to discord. Because if we do not stay and fight, we are not standing up for ourselves, we are not defending ourselves and we are not getting the desired outcome that we want.

I would like to stay, though this should not be confused with a coping mechanism of using avoidance instead of conversation to heal conflict. Avoidance is not the response when dealing with emotional distress in relationships. This aspect shall be discussed in another chapter.

Today, walking away from a situation or a person may be hard, but if it is done with less emotion, a higher rationale and most importantly, without drama, this can lead to a stronger sense of self. Silence is a beautiful response. It is often seen as empty, but in truth, it is full of depth. Silence is the evolution and maturity that is finally setting within the soul. The sound of silence is you rising.

Episode 16
I'm Sorry For Who I Am—Or Was I?

Sorry.

This word was used by me daily for most of my life. I found myself apologising for everything, my fault or not, I would just say sorry. I apologised for when I cared too much, I apologised if I felt too much. I would say sorry for everything I did, for whoever I was and for anything I said. I apologised for being me.

Teens and young adults who suffer from low self-esteem and low self-worth are often apologising for most situations that occur in their lives. For in their minds, they are to blame. They cannot accept themselves as being of value, as they think that they are something to be ashamed of. They tend to self-persecute to the level of assuming every fault to be theirs. The worst part of constant atonement is that the people around you grow accustomed to it. They begin to see everything as your responsibility—and eventually, they come to expect an apology from you, whether or not you're at fault.

I was sorry for who I was; I was sorry for reacting even if the reaction was well deserved. I was sorry for causing any pain even if the response was in self-defence. I was sorry for creating drama even if the abuse was initiated by the other person. I was sorry for dressing in a certain way; I was sorry for speaking in a certain way. I was sorry if someone gave me more attention than I should have gotten. I was just sorry and honestly, it hurt. I knew most of the time, I was just saying sorry because I did not want to lose the person or reduce the feelings between us. I was scared of being without, of being alone, or losing my partner or friend. If only I had known that standing up for myself would have saved me from losing who I was, I might have stopped apologising all the time. Because in the end, I lost more of myself than I ever thought possible.

We often become who we are not out of fear of losing someone, but the price we end up paying is the loss of ourselves. It is not an easy decision—whether to remain your genuine self and risk losing others, or to compromise and risk losing yourself. When we think logically, we realise that we often cling to people out of a fear of being alone. Yet this fear can limit our chances of making new friends and partners and may even cause us to retreat into isolation—risking being labelled as an 'outcast'.

The most important thing is to find the right balance. The faster you accept that you will be disliked by some people, the more you will come to liking yourself. You want to surround yourself with individuals with whom you can be yourself. You want to feel comfortable enough with them even if you have to alter yourself to their likes and their desires once in a while. You will never find a group of friends who are exactly alike. You will find a group of individuals who actually accommodate to one another and also adapt to each other to ensure that as a group, they share opportunities to create wonderful moments and experiences. This applies to relationships as well. In a one-on-one relationship, both partners consistently accommodate and adapt to each other. If you are looking for equality or if you are striving for your partner to think like you and be like you, then you're actually setting yourself and the relationship up for doom. As discussed earlier, if you spend most of your time in the relationship telling your partner how to think and act, you will neither get to know them, nor will you ever have the opportunity of being in a relationship with the genuine version of who your partner is.

There is a distinction between what we are speaking about here and when you are in a situation where there is abuse or signs of sincere disrespect. At that point, it is important to understand the situation and weigh the consequences of your reactive behavioural pattern.

Saying sorry and asking for forgiveness when there is no need or when there is just fear of loss, can impact your well-being on a great level.

Being sorry for who I was chipped away at my inner being in ways that were unimaginable. I saw myself as an aggressor of all things bad, and as a person causing strife in everyone's life. I found myself in daily situations of dramatic consequences and the toll it took on me, physically and mentally, was chaotic. I had no peace—internal or external. My life had become a big ball of drama and I blamed myself for every minute of it. I started to drown in my own pity-party.

Multigenerational trauma is not something to be taken lightly. It can exist in intense forms, and is passed down through generations, manifesting as inner child wounds, attachment issues and deep emotional distress. If trauma is not addressed or healed in one generation, its impact tends to intensify in the next—growing heavier with time, unless consciously broken. Combating this and taking control of the domino effect that occurs from untreated trauma and disregard for mental distress can lead to projection upon those whom you love.

The day I accepted that not everything was my fault is a day I remember well. I noticed the impact it was having on my daughter. She would see me as a constant victim, breaking down into tears or staring out of the window with blank eyes. I knew I was slowly drifting into a space of self-spite but I didn't see the potential impact it would have on my kids. I definitely did not want my daughter to think women are and should be victimised to the point of apologising for their whole being nor did I want her to think this behaviour was normal. For it was not, in any way normal to feel sorry for the person you are. If there is constant turmoil in your life, the triggers must be assessed and either discussed or removed.

Being a martyr was not healthy for anyone, not for me and for others who looked up to me. I did not want my daughter, my kids, to suffer the self-persecution I had been through. I needed to change my perception of myself; it was my responsibility as a mother.

I rose to what life needed me to do. I gradually accepted my faults which needed amendment and I also simultaneously embraced the goodness within me as nothing to be sorry about. It was okay to be a little sensitive; it was also fine if I broke down at times. I was beautiful as I was. I began to see my reflection through the eyes of my children, rather than through the eyes of a damaged teen or through the eyes of judgemental and unhappy soul. Thus began the journey of shedding misperceptions, healing old wounds, putting memories to rest and rising to being who I was, without apology.

Unapologetically me.

Episode 17
The Question That Turned Into Me

Love is love broken down into its stages of 'I like you because' to 'I love you despite' and being able to sustain love through these stages ultimately helps you recognise *'The One.'*

This is the journey of love and if you manage to find yourself striding through these phases as seamlessly as possible, you may have just demystified love as you know it. I wish I knew this when I was younger. There are so many lessons life imparts along the journey; the only obstacle to imbibing them is you.

When my past relationships ended, I always questioned life and divinity with the infamous, *'why me'?* I felt everything that was happening was unjust, unfair and not acceptable. I gave so much love and effort to those relationships that when they ended, it felt like I'd never find someone to share my life with. I thought I was meant to be alone. In those moments, love felt like just a word, not an action. But I've realised—when I can get through love's ups and downs and still feel whole, that's when I'll know I've found the right person.

And this is life's lesson, harsh as it may be, in the trials and tribulations of completed relationships.

For most human beings, the most important aspect of compatibility is friendship. I say most, as there are individuals who can maintain a relationship without ever considering their partner to be a friend. When speaking to different couples about this aspect, I have been told by a few that the role of their spouse or partner was less of that of a best friend but rather that of a companion. There needs to be a balance.

Friendship is the initial moment where two individuals begin their potential journey towards love, as within this juncture, they may realise they may be more than 'friends'. This period is the stage of attraction. Attraction is a wonderful feeling. It is literally where you wear a permanent smile on your face as you are with the person who makes you glow—physically and emotionally. You cannot think of anything else, you cannot sleep or eat without dreaming of that special person. (Please note some people can even forget to eat and sleep during this phase! Your mind is flooded with thoughts of passion and intense longing to be with your partner at all times.) This particular time is most likely the easiest of all the stages as this is one of the happiest times for the relationship.

As time goes by, the attraction, though yet intense and potentially consistent, tends to lose a little bit of its excitement quotient. Human beings instinctively lose interest (as discussed in the earlier chapter) with time in all aspects, as that is human nature at its best. When we enter stage two of the relationship—attachment, this doesn't necessarily mean that the attraction stage is over, it has subconsciously transitioned to a feeling of attachment. Another term we can give to this is emotional attraction. The first stage is predominantly physical attraction and it is fierce in terms of its magnitude. During emotional attraction, you feel a sense of wanting to commit to your loved one. Here there is a desire to nurture and care for your partner in ways that go beyond physical satisfaction and fulfilling of physical needs. This is the period where you may decide to move in together or get engaged to marry.

This stage is crucial, as this is the time when trust, respect and mutual regard for one another are in the forefront. This is also the most important hurdle to cross, as emotional attraction is where heartbreak can occur. As you decide to take the relationship to the next level, you also begin to envision a future with each other and this future comes with responsibilities and challenges. At this point, lust and love take separate paths. This is the moment when you begin to see the difference between physical attraction and emotional connection—and truly understand whether this person is 'the one'. Many people are unable to differentiate this aspect and, therefore, tend to jump into the new phase only to eventually encounter a failed relationship.

Tips to survive this phase are simple in nature. It actually depends on your ability to think clearly with applied logic and rationale. Clarity in thought gives you the ability to apply reason to why you are with this person and what makes this relationship valuable. Thinking about yourself during this period does not make you selfish—it actually provides a sense of stability and balance to both parties as the longer you are in a relationship that is not viable, the more it will pain once it ends. It is better at this phase to sit down and communicate what commitment means to you and your loved one and see if both of you are on the same page. One of my relationships ended very badly because I decided to ignore this aspect and continued in a connection just because I didn't want to be single. This is a terrible thing to do to yourself as well as to your partner. The emotional destruction it caused led to me feeling a sense of guilt for hurting someone I did care about for my own self-serving reasons.

If I could speak to my eighteen-year-old self, I would let her know that it is healthy to be single, it is wonderful to be in a space where there is no responsibility to make anyone but yourself happy. This, in fact, is a luxury, which as you grow older becomes more scarce an opportunity.

Once you've established your affection and commitment to one another, the phase that follows is actually regarded as one of comfort and ease. This particular stage is where you have entered a comfort zone which as we all know is what us as humans love the most. To be anxiety free and open about who we are with without any fear of consequences. Herein, though, lies one of the biggest misconceptions of love and relationship wellness. Comfort is good, but complacency not so much. Openness is wonderful, but criticism and constant nagging, is again not a good thing. Wanting to do what makes you happy—lovely. Disregarding what makes your partner happy—not really. And finally, the nail in the coffin, is finding yourself distracted with the stressors of daily life, at the expense of your loved one's time. So how does comfort and ease end up being a stage of disappointment? Because this is the moment where real life sets in. Physical and emotional attraction exist, but they are not priorities anymore.

Making it through this phase is difficult but not impossible. Love is like life. You create it, you must nurture it and let it evolve as naturally as possible. Sometimes though you get sidelined and things just tend to spiral out of control. Every situation not resolved results in angst, strife and eventually resentment. It is normal for disappointment to lead to a domino effect of pain. The idea here is to grasp hold of the circumstances and try to not become a victim of them. At this juncture, you as an individual and you both as a couple, must clearly identify the means required to save your union. There are multiple routes one can take, inclusive of therapy and support groups.

Some couples enjoy commencing date nights and/or creating a daily time schedule dedicated exclusively to them alone, without the distraction of social, professional, familial and predominantly 'technological' commitments. Once you have managed to overcome this stage of your journey of love, the end result is one of bliss. The course you choose must be one that is agreeable to both parties in order for the process to be successful.

To many of my couples, I suggest a technique that I've found effective: dedicating time to one another and writing down five non-material desires from each other. If, after completing this exercise, they still sense unhappiness, then it may be time to consider other options. Yet, more often than not, simply following through on what was written helps both partners find themselves back in sync—returning to a place of understanding and connection. Sometimes it is in the smallest gestures that we discover the greatest joy.

Whichever path works for you, it is important that you take the step towards it, because most relationships will have to endure this time period and surviving it is deciphering love in its truest form. The final phase in the evolution of love is true commitment. At this point, you have now felt the beauty and the beast of this wonderful thing called *amore*.

Commitment at this phase is real, raw, pure and if I may say, it is the time when you can say you feel 'true love'. Trust has been tested, respect has been earned, nurture has been established, support is unwavering and the fear of loss and the insecurity of abandonment, has decreased.

It is here that individuals begin to live their relationships to the fullest. This is not a phase that is age-related; it is agnostic to age and to the label. You could be live-in partners, you could be exclusively dating or you could be married. This is the time when you are secure with one another and here is where you must begin to maintain independence and give space to your partner to fulfil personal needs which may not include you. I always say that this is where you allot 'freedom with trust'. But even through all these not-so-common factors, you find a middle ground which makes both partners happy. Successful relationships give each other the space to grow independently and indulge in what each of them enjoy, as this simultaneously brings the partners closer together.

Episode 18
Performing Love, Losing Myself

Expectations can be the sole source for misery in a person's life. We all have expectations. I expect, you expect, we all just expect. And this is possibly the most simple yet complex learning lesson that life has to offer.

Expectation has been my partner, stuck to my hip, through most of my life. No matter how many times I told it to fuck off, it simply would not leave my side. It seemed as though it was bound to take me to my grave, and literally so. With my innate nurturing personality traits, I would over-extend myself towards ensuring the people around me were pleased and happy. This constant upkeep tended to not only drain me of my energy levels, keeping me continuously in a state of managing both mine as well as other's emotions. Eventually, it would take me down a slippery slope of exhaustion and frustration. I would forget my needs and would forsake my inner happiness to appease those around me.

Keeping up with people's expectations was only part of my challenge, for with that also came my expectations of people. Now why did I also expect? Well as human beings, this is just within our nature. We are creatures of want and desire and simultaneously, we want to please as well. What we fail to understand is that expectation feeds bitterness. If we desire to live a life free of vexation, we must detach ourselves from the basis of expectancy.

My life was a series of disappointments, but what I would learn later in life was that the cause of this disappointment was more due to my perception. At the time, I was convinced that I was being taken for granted, being an option for those I considered priority, and not being given what I deserved in terms of both treatment as well as needs. If I behaved in a certain manner with others, why could they not bestow the same amount of love, care and attention towards me? I would see my actions as being ones that needed reciprocation. And this was the message I needed to hear. It took me time to realise that if I viewed my actions in this manner, then it defeated the whole purpose of them being deeds of love and care. They were then measures stemming from selfish desire and a seeking of attention. And this was not who I wanted to be. Kindness to me is sexy, compassion is cool, humanity matters and then comes the rest. I knew my whole being blossomed from goodness and I didn't want that compromised in any way.

You could say that I believe in love because of the way I love. Now in itself, the statement is one that should cause calm within you as well as a peace of mind, knowing that it is about you not receiving but rather giving. But of course, as I said the human psyche is one where what you give out, you want in return, maybe not in the total amount you bestow, but at least marginal reciprocation. But here is where we need to alter our cognitive response to our actions of giving. The aspect of giving is selfish even though many of us look at it as a selfless act. Because there is as much of a feeling of positivity when we give and most of the time we are giving to make ourselves feel better even though it's just an act to make the receiver feel good.

In many ways, this also gives us a sense of superiority complex where we feel that we are able to provide and, therefore, maybe in our minds, we are superior? This is just food for thought: when we give, we should focus on the act itself, for the moment expectation enters, the spirit of giving is diminished.

The whole aspect of expectation and expecting less from others is a process which takes time to adjust to. I do not subscribe to the view of deleting all expectation from your life, as I believe strongly in respect, trust and dignity. And these are all aspects which all individuals have a right to. Hence I do expect this form of treatment. And this goes without discrimination. Part of my rising from the damages was self-educating my mind in areas which needed a new sense of perception. I had to alter the way I thought about myself, but I also had to rewire the way I perceived life in general. And this was a whole independent journey in itself.

It is the transition and cognitive perception, transforming the concept of reciprocation in the form of being an expectation to rather being an unexpected act of gratitude. Appreciation and gratitude are truly the most meaningful when they are proactively performed rather than reactively. And this thought alteration betters the quality of life to a great degree.

Episode 19
One Love, One Soul—Or Just A Story We Tell?

Monogamy is manmade; it is a phenomenon created by mankind alone. That is not to say polygamy is ethical, moral or acceptable. Polyamory is a subject which needs a chapter of its own. It just means that when it comes to the soul, when it comes to divinity, when it comes to mythology, the essence of monogamy is an illusion.

There are many individuals who believe in the marvel of soulmates. I was one of them. Every tarot card reading, every clairvoyant I visited and even when I did my own psychic readings, this was always one of the dominating questions. *When will I meet my soulmate? What will it feel like? Will I get tingles up my spine? Will there be signs sent from above?*

I was very excited at the thought of meeting the one soul that my soul had chosen for a lifelong connection. I was anxiously waiting for the one soul that was predestined to be my mate for life. Every person I met romantically, I assumed was that soul. As the years went by, and as my spiritual curiosity developed and began to grow, my understanding of soul connections and karmic bonds started unfolding. And it was a beautiful awakening to a deep and intense new cognisance. The awareness of the elements of multiple soulmates for the many roles that appear in life was truly amazing. As my own soul evolved and transitioned through phases, there were different people that assumed those roles. Each person served a different purpose and vice versa. The intensity that comes with each bond is primarily to teach you a lesson in various ways. That is the special traits of soulmates and their place in our lives.

When we talk about the whole element of finding our soul connection, all of the above comes into context. However, one of the key things we often overlook is that a soulmate may not always be someone with whom we feel an instant connection. Rather, they may be someone who impacts a deeper part of us—someone whose presence shifts something within. Just like human relationships, soul connections can form between people who are remarkably alike or even completely opposite. The soul has connection with others for the same reason. What I mean by this is that our souls also have a certain DNA and that is why we say that our souls tend to find each other in the lifetime that we are living. And this could be due to a past life connection, as well as an unfulfilled connection where we still have a certain life story that needs to be lived out together. Whether you believe in reincarnation or not, the aspect of souls aligning through different lifetimes is one that is ages old. It is actually quite a beautiful sentiment and whether we believe it to be fiction or nonfiction, souls do have an ability to find one another.

As my spiritual being rose, I understood the hidden value of my soul's connections to other souls. I was consistently learning significant aspects through these bonds. Forgiveness, letting go, resistance, and perseverance are just some of the learning lessons that came with my soulmate interactions. There were individuals in my life that have come and gone and as much as I cherished their presence at the time, I knew they needed to exit for others to arrive. That is the beauty of the soulmate connection—they are not meant to be in your life forever. They are there for a reason, and once that is completed, they may or may not stay. I can say now that when I look at the past, I do not pause there. I glance and reminisce and ponder on the lessons taught and the messages imbibed. I thank each soul for their visit into my journey as without them, I possibly would not be the person I am today. I would not have the enlightenment that I feel today. Sometimes, the bond closes its door completely, but that also is nothing to feel sad about. When it comes to the soul, it knows when a debt is due. It understands that for new souls to enter your life, space must be made—and sometimes, that means certain souls must also leave.

Episode 20
What Are You Trying To Teach Me ?

Life is a four-letter word; need I say more? Profound as it may seem, it comes with an intensity that can break your heart to pieces, mind fuck you in ways that are indescribable and give you sleepless nights in abundance. That is the beauty of life's lessons. Uninvited at best, but that does not reduce the level at which it enters.

I never understood why my life was overfilled with such drama. I was exhausted for most of my early years. There were very few days where I had nothing to worry about. Stress was as much of a companion as strife and struggle were. In fact, there were so many times where I just wanted to escape into solitary confinement as I honestly thought life was out to get me. I would wonder what tomorrow would bring and with what drama the day would progress. People, situations and moments seemed to be exaggerated when it came to me. The domino effect was probably based on my life, as one event would set off a chain of events which would last for days. I didn't realise until much later that this kept happening because I refused to learn my lesson and nip it in the bud.

I never imagined that pain would be a mechanism to educate me or to help me become a better person. We view pain as nothing positive but rather a negative emotion that can only be that. The truth is though—pain is like a problem. We also view a problem negatively, but if you delve into the true essence of what a problem is, it is actually a catalyst to improvement. It's only when a problem arises that we begin to seek alternative ways of resolving it—turning to deeper solutions and applying them to our lives. And that, I realised, is what my pain had been trying to teach me all along. It wanted me to learn important aspects which I would have never been able to accept unless it came through pain and struggle.

I was that person—the one who would only accept correction when reasoned with, not when shouted at. The one who would love endlessly if shown even the smallest trace of affection. I was the one who endured torment without question, until I was completely broken. Though this may have appeared to be kindness and compassion, in truth it was the making of emotional baggage that would one day have exploded—had I not reached the spiritual realisation that pain is part and parcel of life, and that it is also meant to heal.

Slowly as I embarked on the journey of self-acceptance through spirituality, I came to accept that the life bestowed upon me had a domino effect—though a meaningful one. A series of interconnected experiences, each leading to the next, designed to teach me some of the most valuable lessons I would ever be blessed with. The biggest lesson being that these experiences were lessons and not life sentences. As the years went by, I began to surrender to all the pain of the past and usher in new perception on life and welcomed the profound lessons of the future.

When we say that we don't have to go through life, but rather grow through it, we must also acknowledge that pain is often the catalyst for that growth. It is through discomfort and challenge that transformation truly begins. Just as we say a problem is a catalyst for improvement, we can say that pain is a doorway to evolution. It is only through pain that we address certain elements. Had we not felt them so deeply, we might never have begun the work to process and heal them. And with every episode of processing, we are actually going through a transformation without realisation. As earlier stated, it is not about being a better human being with every day that passes. It is about being a more involved human being with every day that passes. As long as we are growing mentally and emotionally, we are on a linear path to becoming the version that we are meant to be. It is stressful to strive to become the best version of yourself, and I don't believe this is an endeavour anyone should take on—for the very idea of 'being the best' is a cognitive distortion.

The whole aspect of being the best is highly subjective and there is no real comparative analysis to this point. In fact, it is more so about being the version of you that is the most satisfying in that given moment. For this is truly the most genuine reflection of the *'best'* version of you. Perfectionism in itself is flawed. This particular philosophy will only bring you confusion and constant disappointment. Our biggest achievement is not to be perfect, but rather to be content with our imperfections. Because only if we are imperfect, are we able to appreciate our humanness and accept our real selves as we are.

Episode 21
Words I Swallowed To Keep The Peace

Don't speak, don't raise your voice, don't interrupt—young ladies are meant to be docile, fragile and silent. Just keep quiet. The mental health impact on South Asian women based on culture and conditioning can be quite significant. As a woman of Indian descent, my whole identity is and has been influenced by the traditional teachings of remaining silent. If something doesn't concern you, there's no need to offer an opinion—or even a fact—on the matter—that is what I was told from a very young age. A well-behaved teenager does not get involved in adult-related conversations and they do not speak on taboo or controversial topics. And this applies to relationships as well. You are not supposed to talk back to your husband, your partner or your partner's family. And God forbid the volume should rise—whether out of passion for a cause or anger at the way someone treats humanity. No, my job was to look pretty and nod.

But that was not going to happen. Nor was I going to allow myself to be that person. As I've said before, I feel deeply. For me, to ignore societal or individual mistreatment—or the perception of issues relating to my rights, which have so often been treated as a privilege or even questioned as basic human rights—goes against my moral compass. And if that made me a loose cannon, so be it. I was viewed as the girl who would mouth off if triggered. I was also labelled as imbalanced, crazy, reactive and *jungli* (the hindi equivalent of a wild one). At one point, it did get to me and I found myself refraining from voicing my opinion and restraining my thoughts in the hopes of assuming diplomacy. In all honesty, it lasted only for a couple of months. As a woman, I wanted to speak out for myself, for those who needed it, and for other women who were suffering in silence; as a human being, how could I not stand up for humanity and as a person? It would not be justifiable for anyone to allow exploitation or encourage maltreatment. I just could not conform to what those around me expected. Even if they were my own family.

I agree, maybe I could have been less 'loud' when delivering arguments, and possibly less 'argumentative' when sharing them, but overall, I was not going to keep quiet for the sake of my image.

I could not, would not and honestly should not be silent when witnessing conversation or acts of violation or discrimination.

We must rise, we must say what is unsaid, we must voice out as loudly as we can and we must speak. Sometimes, the greatest growth comes from the 'Un(s)'—unbecoming what you were 'trained' to be and in this case, it was un-silencing the self. There is a point where you realise you have to stop living other people's stories and to put all things that do not resonate with you to rest. For it's those ideas, beliefs, philosophies that impact you, because they are not your thoughts, they are mere manifestations of those around you. Unsilencing your belief system and unleashing it into the world leads to a profound paradigm shift within your own mindset. It is amazing how quickly the mind will adapt to transactional changes made by what you say and what you *put out into the universe.* Your central nervous system will echo internal and external signals that will make your body, mind and soul feel free.

As discussed earlier, a lot of growth doesn't come from the learnings, but rather from the unlearning; from the conditioning and finding yourself and your voice. The main issue at hand is to understand the balance between what you have to say and how you decide to say it. In addition, the moderation comes from what you were trying to say and the message that you are trying to enforce. Speaking out effectively comes with three factors: tremendous listening skills, active comprehension skills and negotiation skills.

It's important to understand the difference between a privilege and a right to recognise that many privileges have now evolved into rights. However, it's equally important to realise that with these rights come a certain power: the power to manifest change. Change that allows individuals—regardless of gender or belief—to exist in ways that were never permitted before.

Episode 22
I Was Never Meant To Carry It All

Sometimes, I wonder if the reason I could not maintain silence against those who violated me was due to the fact that I myself felt victimised. Whether it was my partner, lover, friend, family, colleague or peer, I found myself in multiple situations where I chose to ignore discrimination and disrespect only because I did not want to lose that person from my life. So I compensated for my lack of being able to defend myself by standing up vigorously for others.

This was not healthy either. Most of the ways I reacted to situations in my life were unhealthy, for both me as well as the others involved. For it not only fed their toxic behaviour, but it also allowed them to get away with unjustified actions. In the process of ignoring their conduct, I started losing myself, my self-worth and my self-respect. And as we know by now, this was a vicious cycle which played its role in my life for a long time.

It took me many years to uncover the underlying root cause of why people allow others to abuse them. And the final truth that comes with this insight is quite sad. We do it because we fear loss. What we fail to understand is that the biggest loss that any of us can face is the loss of self—and the loss of all aspects related to the self. For as this loss is suffered, human beings deteriorate to the point of utter self-destruction. And this is literally the greatest damage that one can inflict upon oneself.

I had to change; I had to rise above the nonsense I had grown accustomed to bearing, even if it meant facing potential loneliness. Today, I can actually say, with utmost confidence that cutting ties and distancing from those who showered me with insults, judgements, disrespect and abuse under the pretence of false love has been one of the greatest achievements of my life. I gave so much importance to 'history' of relationships and years spent knowing someone that I forgave any misdeed on the basis of a deep past. What I needed to learn was that the past was exactly that—a place where things need to be put to rest. For sometimes carrying those burdens with you can manifest unnecessary stress in the present.

The loss of any relationship, or any person, is in pretence the death of that particular relationship. Whether it's the loss of a friendship, the end of a partnership, a breakup, or estrangement from family, the body grieves just as it would if the person had died. The pain is real and so is the mourning. For you, this particular loss is the death of that individual. This does not mean that you may never reconcile. It just means that in that given moment, this is what you feel. The phrase *'you are dead to me,'* exists for this particular reason.

Many individuals try to heal the pain of this loss with logic and that is where the intensity increases and the loss is amplified. Emotional pain requires emotions to heal it. The most important thing here is to feel the loss to the point where the loss does not take over. The spiritual understanding that their time with you in this lifetime has come to an end can offer some sense of peace. However, the most important part is allowing yourself to grieve—grieve them fully—knowing that, in the present, they are no longer walking alongside you. By telling myself that my soul's time with them was over—that my lesson from them was complete, that my debt to their soul had come full circle, and that their time in my life was finished—I found some form of consolation. Yet, more important than this reasoning was the need to feel it in order to heal it.

The past moments are to be cherished, however, not remembered. The future is meant to be left alone without any thought. The only way to manifest a more peaceful sensation is to focus only on the present.

Episode 23
Wounds That Grew Feathers

Time heals all wounds; this infamous saying that supports so many of the wounded through their pain—gives hope and faith to heal. My scars were no different. They bled into wounds which stayed with me for many years. For me to ignore the past and move on to the present was one of the most difficult aspects I needed to imbibe. I always felt that when we are damaged by pain, whether self-inflicted or caused by another, we are meant to hold on to those moments as reminders not to be hurt in the same way again. For it is only then that we remember to pause, step back and prevent ourselves from becoming vulnerable to the same hurt again. But that does not necessarily apply when we talk about situations such as loss, rejection or even the possibility of failure. The wounds that eventually may fade do not completely disappear. I was supposed to look at them and remind myself of what it felt like—and how it should never feel that way again. However, something unusual happened, I began to grow and I began to evolve and this led to a totally different mindset.

***

Scars come in a variety of forms, shapes, sizes and depth. Just like you have multiple degrees in burns, you can face trauma at various levels with life lesson wounds. Today, I find myself grateful for the situations that once wounded me, as those very experiences shaped my character in profound and lasting ways. I will not deny that there was pain associated with each—for that is what damages an individual. However, the rise from an abyss of struggle brings with it an amazing strength and perseverance to become a survivor. And when you resurrect, you come with a new perspective on life, a phenomenal superpower to know what energy you will allow into your space and the most astounding bubble to protect you from further breakage. I was scarred and damaged. I lost a lot of my strength; I cried many tears but I would not be who I am today if I hadn't endured all those things.

I am not ashamed of my scars, I am not embarrassed of stating openly that I have been scarred. I am not a victim; I am a conqueror. My scars tell my story—not as a reminder, but rather as a mark of triumph. I can say I have lived and I can proudly say that my failures, my rejections and my challenges have made my life more meaningful, for I have grown.

The thing that we fail to pay attention to is the fact that emotional scars are very similar to physical scars. They are ugliest when they are actually healing. When we look at that wound which is raw and fresh, it's still a sight one can bear. But it becomes most gruesome during the healing—when the scab begins to form, a crusty layer pulls together and sometimes, it bleeds even as it mends. Our scars become the most intense when we are processing them; when we are feeling the pain in order to overcome it.

Just as physical wounds heal to form new skin and fresh cells, emotional wounds are meant to foster a renewed mindset and a revived sense of energy. With each wound, and with each scar, you become a new version of yourself. A version that might have been born through a painful experience, but that version is a stronger you and if you are lucky—a product of a life changing moment.

> *I am scarred, but my scars make me a new woman; the new me and I love her madly.*

Episode 24
Lit From Within

Passion. It is my guiding force which takes me through most of my life with intensity, in all aspects. I can literally say I am so passionate in whatever I do, that the temperature rises to levels of potency. I can never imagine myself doing anything half-heartedly. And that is why my spirit colour is Crimson.

Desire is a strong aspect of my life. Lust to me is not defined alone by intimacy and sexual want. To me lust goes beyond, into the desire for fullness in all that we do. I lust life in its most passionate way. My soul craves to take as much from life as I can. I want to embrace it in the deepest manner, allowing it to take me, teach me and love me as well. To truly live, the mind must stop separating love and lust—for in many ways, they are deeply intertwined, two expressions of the same longing. As I rose, as I grew, I began to understand that love and lust are impressions of desire and cannot be defined independent of one another.

If you feel love ends where lust begins or lust ends where love begins, then you are in a state of disillusion and are setting yourself up for damage. You must ignite your inner desire and manifest the passion that lays dormant within. And to do this, you must not suppress lust, but instead, you must allow it to surface. We have all been programmed to believe lust is sin, but to me, my feeling of lust is not to overpower or overcome but to create a love in its most special way.

There is a fire within me that burns bright and I have known this for most of my life. This fire has caused me to self-destruct in many ways, as I tend to burn out at times, but it has also enabled me to create my mark in the things I choose to do. You need passion to be someone who wants to be remembered. I want to be that person who has given her heart, body, mind and soul to all things desired.

***

There are two paths in life—your purpose and your passion. Your purpose is your calling: what your mind is meant to do and your passion is your desire: what your soul is meant to do. If you are lucky, you will be able to live one of these paths to its fullest and find fulfilment in your lifetime. And if you are truly special and open to life's greatest blessings, both paths will amalgamate and you will find your purpose and your passion culminating into one.

Generally, they say the first part of your life is based on living your purpose and the latter part is to live out your passion. Either way it is important to find peace and satisfaction in whatever you choose to do.

> *I love life and I lust life; I give to it as much as I take from it and that is why I can say I love life as much as I am in love with life.*

Episode 25
She Is The Calm Of The Night As The Moon Dims Its Light

My spirit flower is the lotus. I have always connected to floral creations. From its large pink-hued petals to the way it graces the pond, perched on a throne of green buds like the queen of all flowers, I find myself deeply drawn to its elegance and quiet strength.

To me, the lotus holds many meanings, aside from its beauty and will. I have grown up exposed to its sacred being. Our Hindu Goddess Laxmi—the Goddess of fortune, wealth, love and beauty—is depicted as sitting or standing on a lotus pedestal, as well as holding a lotus in her hands. Here the lotus symbolises spiritual liberation and self-knowledge. Hence, the lotus in its depth carries a sense of self-evolution as symbolism.

The lotus is a flower that blossoms through mud, through filth, through dirt. Each challenge in my life has triggered a unique growth spurt within my inner being as well.

Could I say the difficulties I have faced are equivalent to filth and dirt? Maybe, maybe not, but they have been moments of strife which made me question not only my only self but also humanity as a whole.

The lotus is a flower symbolising new beginnings. The lotus also is a flower of endings. For any new beginning, there must be an ending. My life is a series of endings and beginnings. I was 7 years old when my father met with a near fatal car accident. The fear of losing my idol, my first love, my entire world—my father—left scars so deep that the panic lingered until I finally began to recover at 14. I was in constant fear of losing one of my parents and had chronic nightmares and panic attacks over the years. I was unable to overcome the idea of abandonment and this was the ending of stability and security and the birth of a young girl who was scared to be alone.

They say trauma inhibits cognitive processing in ways where our EQ is purposefully *dumbed* down by ourselves. We stop relying on ourselves for support, neglect our own emotional system and slip into an unhealthy pattern of co-dependency on others. In addition to this co-dependency, we begin to allow others to treat us in ways that we are familiar with—often mirroring patterns and behaviours our systems have been exposed to in the past. And if we look at these ways and mannerisms, we can actually identify them as being either toxic or traumatic. Thus, the co-dependency we develop from trauma and emotional shutdown often leads us into relationships that come at the expense of our own well-being.

It was at this point in my life where I developed a dependency on ensuring I always had someone by my side. This would be at the expense of my own self at many times, as I would allow indignities just to hold onto the friendship, the relationship and the person. I would know in my heart that this particular bond was not healthy nor was it 'good' for me, but I would yet persist in keeping it alive.

When we are young, we are unable to process how pain can

be powerful and how painful episodes can actually manifest into strength. At that age, having someone by our side who paints us as strong feels like a source of strength—because their presence offers comfort. But in reality, it can be a weakness, as it masks our own need to build that strength from within. It took me a long time to realise that a toxic presence was a greater insult to my own self-being than a difficult absence. Because again at this point, our emotional wellbeing takes a backseat to our physical requirement.

As I've said, life is not easy, but it is simple. And life's message through the lotus is quite special. They say the lotus emerges from negativity. With time, I would say each moment of pain made me slightly stronger even if it momentarily, weakened me.

I know this is hard to understand as it is conflicting in nature, but the fact was, as my mind and heart weakened, my soul evolved. Unfortunately, it just happened to physically reawaken to transform later in life. The rise from being buried began in my mid-twenties, with the final evolution not arriving until I was forty. As I've said, it has been a journey of endings and new beginnings. Though at times I did succumb to the torment, I remain grateful that in one way or another, I always found some form of solace—enough to prevent any further self-harm.

As we begin to recognise how pain transforms our emotions, we begin to understand the connect between the mental system and the physical system. Think of it in logic terms: the more we work out our muscles, the stronger they become, even though they feel weak during the working out process. In much the same way, the more we allow ourselves to truly feel our emotions, the stronger they may seem at first. But in feeling them fully, they begin to lose their hold over us—and we gain power over them. It is through pain that this process unfolds, allowing the emotions to work their way out.

Pain a four letter word, I do feel weak,
From it stems strength, but not easy to see.
With time I appreciate how this four letter word,
Can transform to be my wings, making me fly free like a bird.

Episode 26
I Was Never Really Gone

A goddess has risen, from the depths of the soul, where acceptance has manifested into abundance. A woman no longer scorned or jaded by past experiences, rather to emerge with beauty and grace and a sense of gratitude and inner peace. This woman was finally me.

Pride, ego, arrogance; defence mechanisms which are inhabited by most individuals when dealing with any insecurity, pain or challenge take control only if you allow them to. I used to wear them as my shield. They were my armour to prevent any further damage to my mind, body, heart or spirit. I needed to accept that no one could damage me unless I allowed them to. I also needed to internalise that these mechanisms were causing further damage to my inner being. No matter how strongly the voices speak to you—whether from your gut, your mind, or the depths within—if you cannot rise to evolution, you will remain stuck in limbo, trapped in a vicious cycle leading nowhere. I would and could say that my flight to enlightenment was one of the most fascinating experiences of my life. As it was self-learned and self-taught and it was through self-persecution that I finally found my real worth. I know this sounds bizarre and it was. I was only able to evolve once I had beaten myself down to the core. I needed to hate myself to love myself. It is only when you identify your demons and accept them for what they are, that you are able to overcome them. Light emerges through darkness and it shines brightest only after breaking free from it. This was how I rose to evolution. I felt more angst and pain in the months closest to my acceptance of myself, my life, the people within it and of all the multifaceted layers that come with a life lived to the fullest. A goddess phenomenon is merely unleashing the elements that can pain you, shedding the layers of what can affect you, until the only part of you that is bare and open is love. Love for yourself and love for those around you.

Venus has risen and what I feel is relief. Relief through exhaling a sigh knowing that no one can pain me any more, as I am not responsible for them or their actions. No one will be able to exude a reaction from me, as I am not feeding their entertainment factor and no one has control over my emotions, as my emotions are now only answerable to me.

Let me remind you again that there is a clear distinction between reaction and response. Being responsive rather than reactive is a paradigm shift for your entire system, affecting you not only physically and mentally, but also shaping your approach to life's challenges and your interpersonal relationships. The inner goddess within us has the strength to understand that emotions are meant to be felt and thereafter processed on an external level. Rather than internalising any given situation, we perceive it through our third eye or our external lens. This level of self-control creates an inner balance, making thoughtful response our primary action while significantly reducing impulsive reactions. So, how do we achieve this? The idea is to separate the larger issue into smaller parts. Are you upset with what your partner is saying or are you upset with the tone that they are using? The context would make you respond; the tone would make you react. At this given point are we more concerned with the words or are we more concerned with the style of delivery? Within the similar manner, your inner self a.k.a. your inner goddess becomes an advisor of sorts.

Your inner goddess is your mentor, your emotional mentor in many ways. In her is the superpower to compartmentalise the world and situations into aspects that require a response and understanding on when a reaction may be necessary. It also helps to alienate the self from any untoward energies.

My ability today to walk away from situations; my silence that keeps me from reacting to absurdities; my focus on becoming who I know I am; my acceptance of life and all its lessons and my shield to protect me from negativity are some of the most beautiful products of the rise of my inner self.

My darling, now you know what to do,
The path lay forward with moments anew ...
Rise my love, never go back to what broke you
Death, a paradox, an end that begins

One moment to lose, another to win
Into anew as you leave the past behind,
The future awaits you, a new life defined

Episode 27
Is This Love Or A Memory?

Love is as much an illusion as it is not. That is the paradox of love. What makes love real? There are countless definitions, each breaking it down into its many intricacies. To me, this is the true beauty of love—an emotion, and a noun as much as a verb. We seek to see love, to feel it with a belief that it is what we know it to be. Herein lies the irony of it all—love can either make you or it can break you. To me, love was always supposed to be a happily ever after fairytale. Then again, we all know how much tragedy each fairytale journey includes. It is a wonder we even crave love given the tragic tales associated with loving someone.

My journey of evolution is best described as my desire to understand and decode love in all its forms. I needed to understand why love had to hurt as much as it did for it to feel real. And finally, I understood that it was not supposed to.

Love was the belief that my inner being was trying to convey. My soul was speaking to me in ways that I could only comprehend at this stage in my life. I began to free my mind from the blocks that hindered my openness, allowing me to accept what was fated—a true love created for me by a power far greater than I could ever imagine. And what made this love authentic was the realness of it, a love that encompassed many facets and this was the love my soul desired. But the object of love was me. My true love story was about me truly loving myself. For only when I was able to truly love myself was I able to allow someone to love me.

When you spiritually evolve, the soul takes over in many ways, as the voice of reason and as the avatar of your wellbeing.

I knew that where I was, who I was with and the love I felt were exactly right. Trusting the unseen and embracing love's irony reveals the deeper meaning and hidden gifts in life.

That is why I say constantly that it is not about seeking love, it is about feeling love. It is honestly about having that self-love affair with yourself where you can honestly say that your belief and love comes from the way you love. If you love yourself, you undeniably are fulfilling.

Episode 28
The Quiet That Changed Everything

Trusting myself was as hard as loving myself. I always had a sixth sense, a connect to the paranormal of sorts as well. From my infamous ouija board days to holding séances, reading tarot cards and being a spirit whisperer, I knew there was something eerily special about my sixth sense. Sometimes I do ponder in thought on whether it was maybe angels in the sky, spirits I have loved or possibly divinity at its highest that allowed me to stay alive through the moments I felt weakest. As teenagers, we are certainly aware of the gut feeling that arises within us during moments of conflict, distress, temptation and more. The naivety comes from not paying heed to what your inner being is saying to you. That was me. The one that knew what I was about to do was stupid, dangerous, risky, but I did it because I wanted to impress those around me. I wanted people to like me for what I did, for how amazingly 'cool' I was.

Now this is a very normal phenomenon amongst all teens, but for me, what set me apart, was that I was indulging in acts of ruthlessness because I was sad inside. I knew I was sad, but I didn't treat the sadness; I just escaped from it through rebellion.

I was the girl who wore the biggest smile on her face, who was the life of the party, dancing to every beat, singing the loudest, partying the hardest, but only to cry myself to sleep. Because I knew that what I was doing was not making me happy, rather it was just me putting up a façade of who I was to the world.

It is very important to distinguish between stating your case and proving your case. When we're trying to prove our case, we often focus on who we are not, rather than simply stating our case—which is about stating who we truly are. This is one of the strongest lessons your inner voice and your soul will eventually help you learn if you allow yourself the opportunity to be guided.

I wanted to trust my inner instinct and be who I was supposed to be. I just didn't know how. And the only element that did, was my soul. My soul became the guiding force behind all my future decisions: the people I welcomed into my life, the situations that deserved a response, the moments to walk away and the things worth holding onto. Most importantly, it taught me who to forgive, which memories to let go of, what baggage to release and that while history matters, nothing is more precious than you. It took me time, but eventually I needed to accept that the inner voice is me.

I use the term 'soul' as a third party because I do believe the soul is your greatest teacher. As humans, we are born with DNA that uniquely sets us apart from one another. This DNA also carries with it a certain amount of its own 'baggage.' Similarly, our soul, each soul within each of us, independently comes with its own baggage aka 'karma'. What I mean by this is that even our soul has its own unique properties and chemistry. This is why the soul is the captain of our vessel, and the determining factor within all our karmic connections. The soul is the ever-knowing energy force within us that subtly guides us through multiple decision-making situations, challenges and difficulties. Trust the soul as energy doesn't lie.

You knew me better than I know me
You broke through the barrier to set me free
You made me see a version of me true
Rather than the mirror of that's not you …

Episode 29
Tears That Speak

It started with one comment. One quiet thought I shared—nothing sharp, nothing mean. But something in it struck a nerve. And what came back wasn't a conversation. It was a wave of insult—loud, dismissive, cutting. I stayed calm, as I'd learned to do over the years. I breathed through it. I didn't match the heat with more heat.

But then the tears came.

Because I'm human. Because I'm a woman who feels. Because when the people you love aim their hurt at you, it stings in a way nothing else can. And instead of softening, instead of seeing the pain in my eyes, he mocked it. Made fun of me for crying. Laughed at my tenderness.

I can still feel the pain, still taste my tears.

He's in Mumbai, I'm in New York. Thousands of miles apart, but the emotions? They hit just as hard. Pain travels across oceans. So does silence. So does cruelty.

And as the tears run down my face, I am taken back—again—to all the other times. All the times I stayed quiet. All the times I forgave without being asked. All the times I made myself small just to keep the peace. This isn't new for many Indian women. We are raised to endure. To make excuses for men in our lives. To hide our grief in the folds of tradition and silence.

But I don't live there anymore. I don't live in silence. I live in truth now.

Yes, I cried. But I also processed. Because I know how. I've built that muscle. I sat with my pain. I didn't push it away or shame myself for it. I spoke to it gently; the way I would speak to a client—what did this bring up for you? What does this moment remind you of? Where do you feel it in your body?

I journalled. I cried again. I named it: humiliation, hurt, a longing to be seen.

I reminded myself: your tears are valid. Your voice is real. You are not overreacting.

I took a walk. I moved the emotion through my body. I reminded myself of what I know to be true—that his inability to honour my feelings is not a reflection of my worth, but of his own unhealed wounds.

Then I did something revolutionary. I chose not to internalise his reaction. I let it stay with him.

I handed it back, energetically and emotionally, because it's not mine to carry.

I reminded myself that I am raising my son to be a different kind of man. A kind one. One who listens. One who honours the weight of a woman's emotion rather than shrinking from it. That thought anchored me.

This chapter is not written in anger. It's written in truth. In hope. In healing. It's for every Indian woman who's been told her tears are weakness.

It's for every therapist who has to use her own tools in the middle of her own storm.

It's for the girl inside me who was once silenced—and the woman who now speaks with clarity and compassion.

Because this is how we break the cycle: we feel it, we face it, we name it, and then—we heal it.

Episode 30
You Came Wrapped In Karma, Disguised As Love

Karma, what can I say about the phenomenon named Karma. In my preview, I unveiled my relationship with karma, my guiding force in many ways, my advisor and my light. Karma is my soulmate.

I share a love affair with karma, one that shall last through infinity. As I evolved, I awoke to visions I could not fathom had existed. I felt as if I was reborn into a new world where life not only manifested all things wonderful, but the beauty and power of it laid so mystically hidden under layers of frivolous perceptions and insignificance. What I always considered to be relevant were mere illusions. There was nothing to lose, nothing to gain; life is a myriad blessings in disguise. We are only to uncover them as we evolve into becoming the destined human beings we are meant to be.

The raw definition of karma being too good and sees good in itself is very basic in nature. Throughout our lives, we will do good and we will do bad. We will constantly be struggling between doing good and doing things that are not so good. Does that mean we are bad people or that we are not liked by karma and shall be served? No, not at all.

Karma is more about understanding that as we evolve, we may have to undergo challenges and difficulties that will make us into versions of ourselves that are not very nice. The idea is to recognise this and to grow from it. As we encounter our not so nice beings, we must use this as a catalyst for evolution.

Growth comes from breaking patterns that may produce those versions of the self that you would rather not become. It is about disabling the actions that disconnect you from the values that your inner self connects with. At this point, we begin to live a life that we truly cannot even consider our own.

I stopped doing what I believed to be the only way to live. I stopped searching, I stopped fighting, I stopped reacting and eventually, I stopped being stripped by the chaos of someone else's battle. I awoke to a whole new perception. I began to understand that all my indulgence in the fight for validation, the fight for vengeance was an invitation of the karmas of another. Why would I want to bear the burden of karmic balance that belongs to someone else? My ultimate battle was won by merely walking away. This was my greatest lesson taught by Karma. We are not meant to consistently manage and control situations. That is possibly the one thing that will never be in our control.

All of this I needed to learn and I did so through immense amounts of pain, challenges, difficulties and strife, only to discover that what I was encountering was none of those elements. The reason they existed was because I allowed them to. Karma unleashes a new way of thinking within your soul once you accept it in its totality. It is not a mere compass guiding you through the moralities of deeds, but is, in fact, a reflection of the inner you. As you strive to become a better version of yourself, karma will alter its mirror image simultaneously. You are not meant to become a better version of yourself.

You were actually meant to become a more evolved version of yourself. And this is where true existence and purpose lie. You exist for a reason and that purpose resonates within and around you daily waiting to unveil its true essence and beauty. And that is also the unrivalled quintessence of KARMA.

End Face
From Prescription To Poison

When someone is diagnosed with a chronic illness, something that lingers quietly beneath the surface, always threatening to return. Doctors don't treat just the symptoms, they prescribe a full protocol: therapies, medications, interventions. Some are powerful, intense. Some come with side-effects. But the point is to stabilise, and to help the body begin healing itself.

And in the beginning, those treatments are life-saving.

They hold you up when you cannot hold yourself.

You are grateful for them, sometimes even dependent.

But the truth with chronic conditions is this: once the root of the illness is treated, once the body begins to restore its own rhythm, those same medicines can start to harm.

What once helped now hinders.

What once soothed now scars.

You begin to notice the side-effects. The emotional fog, the fatigue, the ache that wasn't there before. And so, slowly, carefully, the doctors begin to taper you off. They wean you from the very thing that once saved you because healing has changed your needs.

Love, especially love born from trauma, is no different.

When we carry unhealed wounds, especially those carved in childhood, we unconsciously seek out people who match our pain. Not because we want to hurt, but because they are familiar. They are the exact emotional medicine our trauma-cracked hearts believe they need. They echo our chaos and so we mistake it for connection. We think this feels like home.

And for a while, it works.

They are the mirror, the medicine, the mechanism for survival.

They help us hold the weight. They teach us what we are carrying.

But then healing begins.

Therapy. Self-reflection. Boundaries. Stillness.

We meet our inner child face to face. And that changes everything.

Because once the core wound starts to close, the people we were once drawn to, those trauma-bonded lovers and friends, begin to feel different. The intensity once mistaken for intimacy becomes overwhelming. The neediness once mistaken for closeness starts to suffocate. The drama we called passion now feels like poison.

Just like medicine in remission, they start to show their side-effects.

Irritability. Confusion. Guilt. Exhaustion.

You feel it in your body. In your nervous system.

And deep down, you know what helped you survive can't help you thrive.

As harsh as it sounds, this is the truth of trauma-based relationships. They served their purpose. They did their job. They were the medicine. But now they are the side-effect.

And healing means learning to let go, not out of anger or bitterness, but with the deep wisdom that love born in survival

cannot carry you into peace.
 So no, the love that was once meant to be is not my destination.
 It was part of the treatment plan.
 The love that is meant for me comes after.
 After the wounds. After the therapy. After the weaning.
 It doesn't activate my trauma. It holds space for my wholeness.

 And that is how pain becomes power.
 Not through holding on.
 But through knowing when to finally, lovingly, let go.

***

Love comes in the form of avatars—they may be individuals, energies or relationships taking us through the emergencies of life, the crisis of challenges and the loss through trauma. We need them and we hold onto them, taking the dose on a daily basis, not recognising how much of our self we actually lose in the process.

But once we let them go, we are free and in order to retain the freedom we must affirm who we are and remind ourselves on a consistent level that the wholeness that we desired comes from within us. And remains there.

Read these Affirmations out loud. Whisper them. Write them down. Return to them.

1

I honour the love that helped me survive, even if I choose to not let it stay.
What helped me then is not what I need now.
I release it with respect for myself, with no resentment.

2

I am no longer available for love that demands my pain in order to exist.
Love should not require me to feel small, unheard or empty.

3

I trust that healing changes what I need.
As I grow, my needs evolve.
I am allowed to outgrow the people I once clung to.

4

I do not owe permanence to anyone who came into my life as a lesson.
Some people arrive as teachers, not meant for forever.

5

I give myself permission to let go without guilt.
Letting go is not cruelty.

6

I am not broken for needing medicine. I am wise for knowing when to stop taking it.
The version of me who reached for that love deserved care.
The version of me now deserves peace.

7

I no longer confuse intensity with intimacy.
Calm is not boring.
Consistency is not dull.
I welcome love that feels safe even in silence.

8

I trust the wisdom of my body and nervous system.
When something feels like pressure, tension, or fear— I pause to listen.
When something feels peaceful, I exhale and I stay.

9

I forgive myself for not knowing better back then.
I forgive myself for needing what I needed
And I thank myself for choosing to heal now.

10

I am worthy of love that does not come at the cost of my peace.
Love that holds me gently.
Love that respects my healing.
Love that sees me as whole.
Because now, I see myself as whole too.

The New Me
Thank You For The Pain ...
You Made Me Who I Am Today

I was broken. Damaged beyond repair as per what I had imagined. I never knew that pain would become my greatest superpower. I could not fathom that shattering into pieces would actually enable the rise of a woman so strong that her greatest weakness would transform into a pillar of growth.

I thank all the people, every circumstance that was intentionally or unintentionally meant to harm me, the multitude of negativity that surrounded me and the individuals whose egos defeated me into despair on so many occasions. Today I will say, I don't love them and I don't hate them. It is because of them that I am who I am today. It is because of trauma that I am what I am today.

Life's biggest learning lesson as I said is tough love. It is not an easy journey of enlightenment and neither is it meant to be easy. Today I can say that with each ounce of pain comes a pound of happiness; the only challenge is to uncover it and then recover from it.

There is a formula to channelling your pain into happiness and that requires processing it through acceptance, letting it be, leaving it to fate and walking forward.

We don't know why we are meant to encounter the elements we do, but I do know that the key here is to accept that they were meant to happen. As I've said, we can never force what is not meant for us and we cannot fuck up what is.

Sometimes there will be no answers to life's many questions and maybe that is the hidden key to joy.

I have always searched for reasons, I have always wanted to know why—why did you treat me that way, why did you not love me back, why did you leave, but I do not want to know anymore. Today I say, maybe it is because our souls had a debt to clear or a lesson to serve and our presence in each other's lives had to come full circle.

In the end, I can say I was meant to suffer those moments, as they ultimately taught me resilience, forgiveness, strength and eventually it resulted in the rebirth of a girl.

There is so much more power in silence, in walking away and even greater strength in letting it be.

It gave birth to a new me—a version even I struggle to recognise at times. But I can say one thing with surety: the calm that accompanies rebirth is beyond anything I could have imagined. I feel peace of mind, a quiet sigh of relief and the gentle inhalation of pure love and positive energy. Most importantly, I feel no hate, no pain, no angst and no regret.

> *Own who you are; own your pain, own your happiness, own your love, own your respect, own your value, own your whole being. For if you own you, there is no one in the world that has the control to hurt you, break you or damage you.*

It takes time, evolution helps you know it,
My Darling, nothing breaks the heart if you own it.

The Soul

My mind, my body, my heart ... herewith ... it is my soul ... it is my self ... it has always been, I just needed to find her ...

And this is my story—my ignorance of the inner guidance that was always present, yet overlooked in my desperate need for acceptance from people and places that, in truth, were inconsequential. Had I known then what I understand now—about the deeper meaning of life and the truth that we are ultimately living for our inner self—my journey might have unfolded in a very different way. The pain of not understanding is far greater than the pain of knowing things that are omnipresent yet hidden. I needed to accept myself, and live for myself. For me, the journey was about learning to love myself.

My evolution led me to my soul, my inner goddess, my inner self, my inner voice, whatever you may choose to call it—ultimately the new Me.

A new Me that was the product of the Me that always existed, within myself.

Through biased experiences, I learned to become unbiased. Through a lifetime of being judged, I grew to be non-judgemental. Through pain, I discovered my strength. The self—the one we so often speak of, yet rarely pause to consider—holds depth and power far greater than we realise.

Our mind guides us to believe that the body comes with a soul, but ever so often, we disregard the self and give power to our mind, allowing it to control us. We tend to feed our mind's desire and we indulge the body ensuring that what we do is based upon what the mind and body want, not what the self needs.

But when it comes to peace of mind, stability of inner being, overall mental wellness—it is the soul—the self that is our advisor. We do not give enough credit to the inner vibes and energies that our true self feeds us daily. We ignore the voices that come from within and write them off as possible paranoia, disillusion and sometimes even imbalance.

My existence was my power, the love that stirs in my soul and I was to ensure as many people sipped from the ocean of this potion.

***

After reading this book, you might ask yourself what is the meaning of this book? What is the author trying to tell us? Why is she sharing all of this pain? What is the purpose? How will her pain help us navigate relationships or lead a better quality of life?

They say the greatest experiences of life will unearth some of the deepest sensations within our system. If it's not transformational, then it's probably not an experience. All of my transformations—painful as they may have been—have shaped experiences that led to profound shifts in my emotional growth. It is this experiential methodology of therapeutic processing that I am hoping will impact those who hear my stories. Stories that include episodes of angst, but also deep healing methods and recovery techniques.

I cannot take away your trauma, just as I was unable to take away mine. I cannot erase what happened just as I could not erase what happened to me. But I can tell you that you can live a beautiful life despite the trauma, despite negative episodes. It is not about deleting moments of your life; it is about leading the life you were meant to lead, regardless of how others have impacted it.

There is a *new you* always within you. There is an *unbroken* version of you always within you. There is a *peaceful* you always within you.

You just need to find her or him.

Pain
It's The Gift Of Thorns

If this book has shown you anything, let it be this: You are not who you were in your moments of pain. You are who you become because of them. Healing is not about returning to who you used to be; it is about stepping into the shoes of the person you were always meant to become.

The spaces between heartbreak and healing, between loss and love, between falling apart and finding yourself—those are the spaces where transformation happens. And transformation is rarely gentle. It asks you to surrender, to trust, to walk through the fire of your own becoming. But in the end, it leaves you with something unshakable: you.

You are the love you've been searching for. You are the home you've been longing to return to. And every scar, every tear, every moment of breaking was not a sign of your weakness but proof of your strength.

So, if you ever wonder whether you are strong enough to keep going, let me remind you: You already are.

This is not the end of your story.
This is the beginning of your power.

Conception

Orgy of the mind, body, heart
Orgasmic eruption of intense art

Justice ... injustice ... poetic lyric culminate to climax
Soul screams to release the impassioned with fire

Verses conceived from the womb of the soul
Painful existence channelled for redemption

Moments unleashed, many buried to be hidden
Return to life into free verse expressed

Conception deliverance, rhythmic rhyme be
Come birth of the sobriquet ... poetically

Shai C.

Poetically

She expressed through words, words written in the silence, in the middle of the night when no one was awake to see her tears, to feel her ache or to see the truth.

Rhythmic motion in lyrics, coming together to communicate the confusion, the suffering, the angst, in the only way she knew how to release. She was broken, broken by the moments that slowly chipped away at her, unveiling the vulnerability within.

A mask worn consistently to shield the true face and held low in fear. She knew there was a lack of love, but she thought it was that no one loved her truly. In the end, she realised that the love she lacked was her own. The love she needed had to come from within. And the love she longed for had always been inside her.

So, she started on a new journey of love—the journey of loving Shai C.

I am Shai C.

I am you.

***

The pain you have felt, I am that.
The rejection you have experienced, I am that.
The love you have not received, I am that.
The abuse you have tolerated, I am that.
The trust that has been broken, I am that.
I am the hope that once felt lost.
I am the faith that struggled to hold on.
I am the silent tears that no one saw.

The loss of you, I am that.
I am also the healing and the surrendering.
I am the rising and the evolving.
I am the resurrected love and the ultimate nirvana.
I am the broken moving towards the unbroken.
I am the validation.
I am the acceptance.
I am the new you.
The new you.
Believe in love ... for the way you love.

Shai C.

Short Verses and Quotes

She spoke with her eyes
Telling stories of love in the wild

Her heart beats to a drum
Rhythmically her own
Her body dances to a melody
Composed by her soul

Her existence is her power
The love that stirs her soul

Bestowed to the one who feeds her soul
She is the wild of the sky as the sun rises to shine

She lived a life of her will
Owning her heart and mind

She wore her scars as wings

Her beauty shone bright
Like a glimmer of light
In the ebony of the night

She loved with a desire so intense
Her passion could set fire to a bed of wet roses

Her love is a weapon
A dagger to the dark
A shield to the light

Her world, a new world of calm and love
No more desire to avenge
Let those who pained her be at peace
She thanked them for making her into the woman she was today

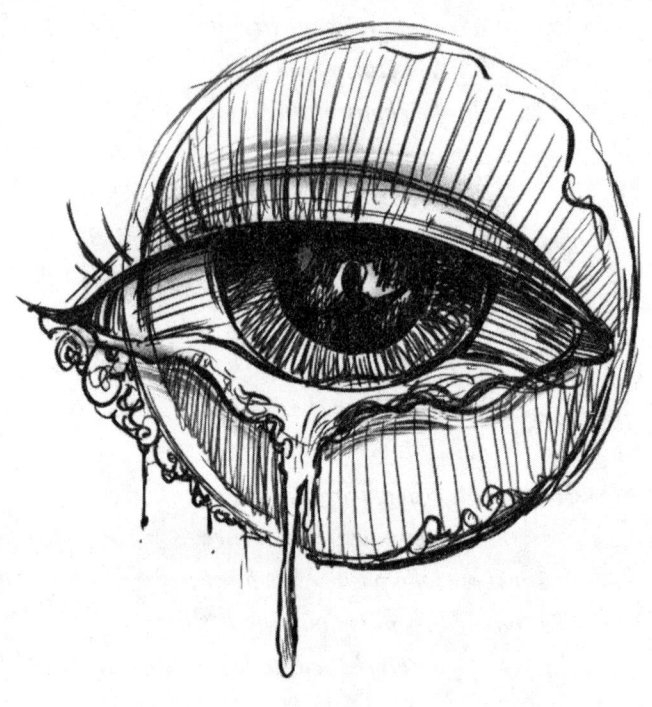

*Pain—a four letter word that taught me so much
Helped me rise into what I never thought I'd become
I left the past behind and grabbed the present by the balls
Cut what I needed to let go of and embrace the rest of it all
There is no more angst or need for validation
No need to react, no need to respond, just silenced patience
Pain, you're a four-letter word, and fucked me, you did
But I want to thank you, for the new me is
someone I'm glad I have met.*

xoxo - this is my fight song –
Shai C.

BEYOND MEANT TO BE

1

As a South Asian woman growing up in America, I struggled to navigate two worlds. One valued discipline, self-sacrifice, modesty and quiet strength. The other celebrated individuality, self-expression and boldness. To feel love and acceptance, I thought I had to be everything to everyone.

Within the Indian community, I had to be the perfect daughter. The overachiever. The 'good Indian girl' who followed the rules, smiled through discomfort and never asked for too much. And with my American friends, I had to blend in—be likable, agreeable and shine just enough, but never too much.

So I played it safe. I followed the script my parents' world defined as success: an engineering degree from a top school, a high-powered consulting job, a steady relationship. I made everyone proud.

But in chasing perfection and approval, I never asked the most important question: What do I want?

From the outside, I looked like I was thriving. But inside, I felt a quiet ache. I was split into two.

After moving to New York, something stirred—a childhood dream I had never said out loud. I signed up for an acting class. I wasn't a natural by any means, but something awakened in me: freedom. A part of me that had been asleep, came alive.

By day, I lived the life I was supposed to want. At night, I snuck off to acting classes and writing workshops, quietly nurturing the side of me that longed to create, to express, to live more freely. I didn't tell many people. When I did, I was met with confusion or judgement. Slowly, I began to absorb the idea that wanting something so far outside the box I'd been placed in was selfish. Shameful. So I held it in.

Still, I kept going. I worked 60+ hours a week while secretly building a second life—one that gave me breath. I was full of passion—but also full of shame for wanting more. I compartmentalised everything, trying to hold it all together. And then one day, my body said: no more.

I had a grand mal seizure. At work. In front of all my colleagues.

It was scary. But in hindsight, it was the clearest message I could've received: You cannot keep living this way. The pressure to be perfect, to juggle ambition and tradition, to suppress your truth while performing competence—it was unsustainable.

I had to make a choice. I chose acting. I chose me.

Leaving behind my structured career wasn't just a leap into a new profession; it was a leap toward myself. A choice to be honest. To honour my vulnerability. It was deeply exposing. I was stepping out of a world where my identity was validated for fitting in and into one where I had to earn my place by showing up fully as I was, with no guarantees and rejection at every turn.

There are moments that break your heart—when the role goes to someone else, when the script you poured yourself into gets a no. The silence after pouring your heart out. But I'm still going. Not because I have it all figured out, but because I'm finally living in alignment with who I really am.

Motherhood and marriage have added new layers. These days, I feel the pressure more than ever to be everything: ambitious and nurturing, strong and soft, disciplined and present. Sometimes I break. But this creative life grounds me. It gives me energy when everything else feels overwhelming. It's mine. And just as important, I have a group of women I can be real with—people

I can talk to, cry with, laugh with. That kind of support changes everything. And no one can take that away from me.

I've learned that the bravest thing we can do is stop hiding from others, but especially from ourselves. Vulnerability isn't weakness. It's where our clarity lives. It's where healing starts.

But we're not meant to do that kind of work alone.

We need spaces to be real. To say the hard things out loud. We need other women who get it—who carry the same pressures, the same quiet ache—and who can meet us with honesty, not judgement. In those moments of connection, shame loosens its grip. And we remember we're not alone.

That's the journey I'm still on. And while I know my story may not carry the weight of what others have endured, I offer it humbly, in case it helps even one person feel seen.

Thank you, Shalini, for writing this book, for opening up the conversation, for holding space for our stories and for reminding us that being seen is powerful. And that we were never meant to carry all of this on our own.

—Melanie Chandra
Actress, Producer & Storyteller

2

There are books that inform, and then there are books that transform. *Love That Was ~~Meant to Be~~ Meant for Me* is the latter.

In these pages, Shai C offers not just her story—but her soul. With every sentence, she lays bare the complexity of pain, the quiet strength of survival and the unflinching beauty of choosing to heal.

As a medical doctor who walks with others on their journeys of renewal—of skin, of self, of confidence—I have come to understand that the deepest wounds are often invisible. They live in our behaviours, our stories, our silences, our inherited expectations.

Shai C's truth-telling is fearless, yet nurturing. Through her writing, I was reminded that feeling deeply is not a flaw—it is a gift.

For every person who has questioned their worth in the face of betrayal, burnout, or breakdown—this book is a guide back home. And for every healer, like myself, who sees the quiet courage it takes to simply feel—this book is a reminder that there is no shame in breaking, only power in rising.

This isn't just a collection of reflections. It's a companion—a steady, honest voice that walks beside you through the difficult terrain of healing. Within it, we find not only Shai C's resilience, but our own.

Dr Harshna Bijlani
Aesthetic Physician and celebrity skin expert/Founder,
AgeLess Clinic

3

For centuries, women have played the roles assigned to them—willingly, lovingly, or simply because they were expected to. We have been the dutiful daughters, nurturing mothers, supportive wives, ideal daughters-in-law, tireless caregivers. We have worn these roles like second skin, praised when we lose ourselves in them. We are elevated to the status of goddesses—but only when we serve, sacrifice and suppress.

Somewhere along the way, in trying to be everything to everyone, we forgot to be ourselves. We traded our softness for strength. Our fluidity for structure. Our femininity for function. We became Mansi—a metaphor for every woman carrying the invisible weight of perfection. Performing endlessly, applauded silently, breaking slowly.

Why did we let this happen? Why were we conditioned to believe that our worth lies in how much we give, how well we manage, how quietly we endure? Who decided that being a woman meant being everything except our own selves?

This book is not just a reclaiming. It is a rebellion. It is a remembrance of the woman beneath the roles. A voice for every Mansi who forgot that she is more than her responsibilities. It is time we stopped playing the goddess only to please the world—and started honouring the goddess within.

Let's break the norm. And begin again—as women, not roles.

Deepika Gehani
Co-Founder, Lililo
Partner Dhun Wellness

4

As an overweight actor I was only ever allowed angry, hungry or horny as acceptable emotions on screen. But as a human being, I had soooooo many more. Then one-day guilt took a peek when I tried to do more. The effort was shot down and laughed at immediately. Guilt reared its head and became a part of the background that everything was placed against. It festered and it grew, until I only felt FAT! There was nothing else to my existence except my weight. It was the messenger announcing the need to change. Too hurt and completely unequipped to process it, I ran away.

Left to my own devices to figure it out, I decided to work on the outside. The fat, that was responsible for it all. That was my wound, and it was all over my body! No matter how hard I worked, it did not heal. The wound only got larger. What was I missing? The suppressed and repressed inner world!! Yes!! I started with wanting to talk about it but found it difficult to ask. So I started writing. Surprising myself, I wrote pages and pages of everything. Unable to contain it any longer, I painted the walls of my rented house, cried oceans, starved and at time lay listless on the floor for hours. All this because I had started processing everything I had repressed. The beauty was not far. In a while I turned into a beautiful woman with less triggers and more in sync with her abilities and possibilities. Someone who recognised the power of 'Journaling' in self-discovery. I was sorting the inner world out, one sheet of writing at a time. I was accepting and owning all of me.

The size remained, the wound healed and I was finally cast for the power I held within it. The main lead in *Mahi Way* with Yash Raj Films, demanded I show more of my emotions. The Universe had acknowledged the pain I felt through all the processing and gave me an opportunity to test it out. I loved it, the world loved it and Mahi became a beacon of hope for many women who are struggling with the same story.

The Universe is noticing—are you also going from surviving to thriving?

As Pushtie I am healer, yogini, teacher, friend, actress and much more. Yet, through all of this, my path is to help people see the ultimate potential within themselves. To see that healing IS possible! My trick is humour and simplification! I swear like a sailor on the run and love like a new born mother. And somewhere within all of that.. I try to remain HUMAN!

Pushtie Shakti
Actor, Tarot Reader, Life Coach

5

I wish I could say I had the answers. That I found a method, a path, a roadmap. But for me, healing has always been a series of experiments—a long, winding journey of trial and error. And even now, ten years later, I'm still searching for the method that finally makes it all make sense.

The first time I fell in love, I believed—with all my heart—that this was the man. Even now, some days, I still wonder if maybe he was. But love, as I learned the hard way, can be deeply entangled with hurt. And sometimes, it's the person we love most who fractures us the deepest.

We were engaged. The wedding was planned. And just a few months before the big day, something shifted. The man I loved began to take a back seat as his family stepped forward—demanding, negotiating and eventually, asking my family for money. I waited for him to stand up, to speak out, to stop the madness. I thought he would protect me.

I hold three master's degrees across three continents. I come from generational wealth, strong women and an upbringing rooted in dignity and independence. I never imagined that I would be treated like a transaction. That I would be harassed for dowry. That love could look like silence in the face of injustice.

I was in denial at first. My heart refused to keep up with what my mind had started to register. Slowly—over weeks, then months—my love began to collapse in on itself. A quiet shutting down of the heart. A survival mechanism, perhaps. A final surrender.

And yet, here I am. A decade later. Still carrying fragments of that pain. I've sought therapy. I meditate daily. I speak to my wounds with gentleness, trying to see that time as an episode, not as a defining truth, not as a person. Some days, I feel like

I've made it through. Other days, I feel like I'm still stuck in that room where everything broke.

But if there's one thing I know for sure, it's this: I am a work in progress. And progress is still power. The hurt has not defined me. It has shaped me. It has deepened me. It has made me fiercely compassionate and incredibly discerning. And in that, maybe, there's power—not because I rose above it, but because I learned to stand inside it with open eyes and an open heart. That is why *Love That Was ~~Meant to Be~~, Meant for Me* feels so personal to me. Shai's words echo the quiet strength it takes to sit with pain, to soften into it and to slowly, bravely, build something beautiful from the wreckage. Her story holds a mirror to my own—and perhaps, to yours too.

Jagriti Choudhary
Founder Skinyoga

6

Since being born, we women have been conditioned to believe we are secondary to men. But I believe what makes us different is how we have managed to get through life—and it is that journey that shapes us, that gives us strength. That strength comes from our self-belief; from the resilience we quietly build every time we rise after being pushed down. When we face self-doubt, we must think positively, knowing that our success stories are written by the very strengths we choose to highlight. We make the impossible possible because we don't give up—we carry a die-hard spirit within us. We just have to believe it.

There are countless successful women in the world because they made that difference—they never felt they didn't have it in them. They believed in their own power and so they did it. They achieved.

No man should ever be allowed to make you feel worthless, because you are not. You are a woman—emotionally stronger, deeply capable and able to process pain and pressure in ways many cannot. So how can we allow ourselves to be pushed aside or humiliated? How can any man make a mess of our lives unless we allow them to? I didn't. I took on the world with two babies and no support, because I knew I had to—and I did it. And so can you.

Every journey in life has a struggle. It's how we handle ourselves and come out of it that defines us. Move aside the emotions, move aside what makes us weak, and believe in yourself.

In *Love That Was Meant to Be, Meant for Me* I explored how our deepest pain can become the soil from which resilience grows. This moment reflects that same truth—that breaking is not the end, but a turning point. Our wounds, though raw, often reveal strength we didn't know we carried. Through the process of facing what hurts, we uncover a quiet power—not in spite of the pain, but because of it. It is in the unraveling that we begin to rebuild with intention, and in that rebuilding, we find the beauty that endures.

Lubna Adam
Strategic Advisor – Fashion, Lifestyle & Luxury Brands

7

Being guarded by angels, breaking all norms at the age of 17, I knew that to be accepted I had to reinvent myself. Hence, when you make your weakness your strength, you flourish. We do not need validation from anyone, because when you know you are the best, you choose to empower yourself. I turned my girly passion into a career and immersed myself in creating my own path, which was challenging, but like my mum taught me, instead of seeking help from individuals, you should pray and seek help from God. And yes, my prayers were heard. Even today, I request all to wake up at 3:30 a.m. during Amrit Vela and pray for your inner peace and success — you will surely be a winner. Hard work and focus on your goals are enough to silence the people who try to pull you down. Fall in love with your work; your passion and dedication will always lift you above all.

I have recently lost both my parents, my support system, and was in a terribly depressed, lonely situation. But I remembered my mum and dad's teachings—to wake up at 3:30 am— and I felt their blessings and guiding light in abundance. Prayers can cure all pain and make the impossible possible.

I have made my profession my first love, which allows me to bring my feminine traits into a vision of art. My profession allows me to spread so much love and instant gratitude. I pray for peace, happiness, and abundance for all, as prayers are a cure for any situation.

Always do your best—God will do the rest.

Ojas Rajani
Celebrity Makeup Professional

Reflections

Life often feels like a journey without a map, a series of steps taken blindly through pain, hope and confusion. Many of us move through the world feeling isolated in our struggles, navigating the highs and lows of human experience without guidance or a clear sense of direction. We encounter people who manipulate, gaslight and exploit our natural innocence or trust, leaving us with questions that no one seems to answer. All the while, society presses upon us an invisible but powerful set of expectations, urging us to conform, to fit in, to be something other than our authentic selves.

In this profound and poignant book, the author dares to face these universal pains head-on, acknowledging the heavy weight of human experience that so many of us carry alone. With empathy, insight, and clarity, she shines a light on the psychological and emotional realities of living among those who may wound us—narcissists, manipulators, people who see our vulnerability as an opportunity for control. Yet she never leaves us in despair; instead, she offers understanding and a path forward, revealing practical, evidence-based practices grounded in scientific and social research.

The strength of this work lies not only in its truths but also in its poetic grace, in the way the author captures the complexity of our shared humanity. She reassures us that we are not alone in facing these challenges, that our struggles—though unique—are also profoundly relatable. This book serves as a guide and a lifeline, providing generations with the knowledge, tools, and resilience to navigate life's complexities with clarity and strength. Whether you're facing pain, confusion, or the feeling that you don't quite belong, this book is here for you. It's here to remind you of the power you hold, to reassure you that you are not alone, and to help you recognise that, despite our differences, we are all connected in the same shared struggle. Here is a journey toward healing, growth and a deeper understanding of yourself, and the world around you. The struggles you faced were actually stepping stones, and one by one stripping you and exposing the strength you never knew existed, finally you can breathe while seeing the beauty in the pain.

Professor Lisa Mills
LMSW, CASAC

Acknowledgements

This book has been shaped by many hearts and voices and I feel deeply grateful for each one. To Deepika Gehani, Lubna Adams, Melanie Chandra, Harshna Bijlani, Ojas Rajani, Jagriti Choudhary and Pushtiie: thank you for opening your lives and sharing your stories of strength, resilience and empowerment. Each of you has added a unique light to these pages and together you create a constellation of inspiration for every woman who reads this book.

A special thank you to Savio D'Silva, whose beautiful illustration graces the cover. His artistry captured not just an image, but the very spirit of this work, and I couldn't imagine a more fitting introduction to what lies inside.

This book carries pieces of all of you and for that, I am endlessly thankful.